JESUS CHRIST AND HIS CROSS

Books by
F. W. DILLISTONE
Published by The Westminster Press

Jesus Christ and His Cross
The Structure of the Divine Society
The Holy Spirit in the Life of Today
The Significance of the Cross

JESUS CHRIST AND HIS CROSS

Studies on the Saving Work of Christ

by

F. W. DILLISTONE

Philadelphia

THE WESTMINSTER PRESS

Library of Congress Catalogue Card Number: 52-9811

PRINTED IN THE UNITED STATES OF AMERICA

CONTENTS

PREFACE

Nowhere perhaps do theology and devotion come nearer to one another than at the cross. It is hardly possible to deal with the doctrine of the atonement without being reminded of its inevitable implications for life and conduct. Equally, it is scarcely possible to construct a devotional meditation on the cross unless the material has been prepared beforehand by means of careful theological study. Thus the character of any book that seeks to interpret the meaning of the cross will be largely determined by its particular emphasis. It will be neither strictly theological nor strictly devotional but will attempt to emphasize one or other of these aspects for its own particular purpose.

My aim in the following chapters has been to draw upon studies extending over a good many years in the fields of Biblical and historical theology to provide material suitable for devotional reading. I have tried to avoid all technical discussions though I have not hesitated to invite the reader to engage in a careful consideration of certain Biblical passages. There is, perhaps, some repetition of ideas in different parts of the book, but this may not be altogether a fault if the reading of the chapters is extended over such a season as Lent. Those familiar with *The Book of Common Prayer* will find a connection between the themes of chapters II–VII and the propers of the successive Sundays in Lent, but the use of the book need not depend in any way upon such a connection's being consciously made.

Nothing that I have written hitherto has come nearer to my

deepest interests than *The Significance of the Cross,* which The Westminster Press published in 1944. It has been through the encouragement of Dr. Paul L. Meacham of the same Press that I have returned to my original theme in a rather different way, and I am grateful for this opportunity of sharing with a wider public some of the ideas that have helped me as I have sought to go on thinking about the inexhaustible subject of the meaning of the saving work of Christ.

CHAPTER I

THE MYSTERY OF THE CROSS

> " 'Tis mystery all! the Immortal dies!
> Who can explore His strange design?
> In vain the firstborn seraph tries
> To sound the depths of love divine."

The cross stands at the center of the Christian religion. No other symbol adopted during the centuries of its historical existence can compare in importance with the cross. It is the dominating theme in art and architecture, it is the determinative criterion in faith and conduct, it is the impelling motive in devotion and service. Other systems revolve around other symbols — the crescent, the sickle, the lotus flower, the spinning wheel, the sun's disk, the living flame — but Christianity revolves around the cross. Nothing has a right to the name " Christian " that is contrary to or incompatible with all that this symbol represents.

At first sight this appears to be one of the strangest facts in the whole history of the human race. Does not man love life? Yet the cross points to death. Does not man strive for victory? Yet the cross tells of defeat. Does not man labor to establish harmony and concord? Yet the cross produces disruption and discord. Does not man delight in all that is fair and beautiful? Yet the cross suggests all that is crude and ugly. Why should such a symbol have been chosen? Why has it been so jealously guarded and retained? When all allowances have been made for the historical circumstances within which Christianity came to birth, is it not strange that men should have set the cross in the forefront rather than in the background, that they should have been proud rather than ashamed of this sign of ignominy and defeat? Yet there is no denying the fact that when Christianity has lost touch with the cross it has grown weak, when it has renewed its contact it has renewed its strength. This mysterious symbol cannot be forgotten or ignored. It commands attention, and even outside the ranks of organized Christianity there are those who find it a phenomenon of unusual interest. Let us begin by referring to two recent books by distinguished philosophers in which the cross comes up for discussion in a striking way.

I

In her remarkable book *Philosophy in a New Key,* Susanne K. Langer chooses " The Fabric of Meaning " as the title for her final chapter. She suggests that in living our lives we are all engaged in a kind of weaving process. The warp of our fabric is given to us through the common dependabilities and steady patterns of everyday experience. The clocks which provide our context of time, the familiar landmarks which provide our context of space — these are factors in our experience of which we are scarcely conscious but which form essential parts of the warp of our lives. In addition, however, there is the woof, which, Mrs. Langer suggests, is the host of symbolic forms accumulated by man during his journey through history. Words, shapes, signs gather to themselves meanings, associations, suggestions, and are then available for use by the weaver as he seeks to twist the successive threads of significance into the web of his life.

If we are prepared to envisage our human experience in this way, we can then make a rough-and-ready distinction between the hard facts of our daily existence — the ordinary pattern of domestic and business routine with which most of us are familiar — and the more intangible realm of images and ideas, symbols and metaphors, which are associated with outward forms such as words and shapes though not confined within them. It is this second realm that provides us with the " bright, twisted threads " which constitute life's fascination and man's adventure. To explore any part of it is an interesting quest: to examine the significance of those symbols which have (to use Mrs. Langer's phrase) become " charged " with meaning in a special way is one of the most exciting tasks that anyone can undertake.

Among the " charged " symbols of mankind there is one that

possesses an unusual variety of meanings and associations. It is the cross. " The actual instrument of Christ's death, hence a symbol of suffering; first laid on his shoulders, an actual burden, as well as an actual product of human handiwork, and on both grounds a symbol of his accepted moral burden; also an ancient symbol of the four zodiac points, with a cosmic connotation; a 'natural' symbol of crossroads (we still use it on our highways before an intersection), and therefore of decision, crisis, choice; also of *being crossed,* i.e., of frustration, adversity, fate; and finally, to the artistic eye a cross is the figure of a man. All these and many other meanings lie dormant in that simple, familiar, significant shape. No wonder that it is a magical form! It is charged with meanings, all human and emotional and vaguely cosmic so that they have become integrated into a connotation of the whole religious drama — sin, suffering and redemption." So writes this distinguished modern philosopher. She is not writing as an advocate of the Christian faith nor as an apologist for the cross. She is simply commenting on the way in which this highly charged symbol has come to occupy a place of central importance in one field after another of human experience and interest.

Another suggestive approach to the cross and its relatedness to every aspect of life is to be found in Professor Eugen Rosenstock-Huessy's book *The Christian Future.* He claims that the very story of Christianity is " the penetration of the cross into more and more fields of human existence " (p. 165). Reality itself, he considers, can be regarded as cruciform. " Our existence is a perpetual suffering and wrestling with conflicting forces, paradoxes, contradictions within and without. By them we are stretched and torn in opposite directions, but through them comes renewal. And these opposing directions are summed up by four which define the great space and time axes of all men's life on earth, forming a cross of reality " (p. 166).

This idea of the cross as reality he now expounds more fully. In Time man always stands between the past and the future. He is, as it were, facing backward and forward at the same moment, stretched between his origins and his fulfillment. But man also lives in Space between an internal and external world. "So it is that man's life, social as well as individual, is lived at a crossroads between four 'fronts': *backward* toward the past; *forward* into the future; *inward* among ourselves, our feelings, wishes and dreams; and *outward* against what we must fight or exploit or come to terms with or ignore. It is obviously fatal to fail on any front. . . . Yet it is equally obvious that no individual can move adequately in all four directions at once. Therefore life is perpetual decision. . . . Both mental and social health depends on preserving a delicate mobile balance between forward and backward, inward and outward, trends. Integration, living a complete and full life, is accordingly not some smooth 'adjustment' we can hope to achieve once for all and then coast along with, as popular psychology imagines; it is rather a constant achievement in the teeth of forces which tear us apart on the cross of reality " (pp. 168, 169).

Gathering the insights of these two writers together, we may now move into our main theme by saying that man cannot live, or at least cannot truly and fully live, except by carrying on a constant process of symbolization. Through this process the search for meaning goes steadily forward and gradually certain outstanding symbols establish themselves as of peculiar significance. Such a symbol, as Mrs. Langer has shown, is the cross. Not only in Christian tradition but also in the wider areas of human experience the cross stands for strange, far-off, remembered things. But this is no accident. If, as Dr. Rosenstock-Huessy claims, the very nature of human experience is cruciform, if man's whole existence when fully lived is four-fronted, with a tension always persisting between opposite aspects within the whole, then there is, as it were, a cross pattern within man's consciousness which waits for its corresponding cross pattern within the realm of external signs. From every standpoint, then, the cross may be regarded as one of the supreme interpretative symbols of the drama of human life.

II

But is the cross any longer understood? Does it any longer call to the depths of the human situation? Is its symbolic power still recognized? It is not easy to answer these questions with confidence. Let us take, for example, an incident recorded by Philip Mairet in *The Frontier* of June, 1950. " Just about ten years ago, a young French workman was hurrying into the country out of an industrial town which was swarming like an overturned anthill. A compatriot of another class, also fleeing from the invaders, got into conversation with him; and as they passed a wayside crucifix the young laborer inquired, ' What is that? ' He had no idea, and it was no light task to enlighten him, for this inhabitant of a factory area in cathedral-conscious France turned out to be as totally ignorant of religious knowledge of any kind as many of his opposite numbers in Britain are said to be." Such an example is all too representative of a situation in our Western world in which the cross, sin, and salvation have become virtually meaningless terms. No longer, it appears, is the cross regarded as an essential part of the symbolism of human life.

On the other side we may set a personal experience recorded by the novelist J. B. Priestley in a broadcast during the early part of 1950. While journeying across England on a tour of investigation and inquiry, he came to Coventry with its bombed-out cathedral. He describes his visit to the roofless ruin in these terms: " We stepped into light instead of the familiar ecclesiastical dusk. . . . The city outside had vanished and was forgotten. There was nothing but this ruin, rosy but infinitely solemn, and the vast pearl of the afternoon. It was very strange, very beautiful. In some such roofless glowing place, under some desert sky but yet with these familiar symbols about them, the early Christians might have worshiped. We moved forward, slowly, not talking, making as little sound as possible. And then it was not only strange and beautiful but also deeply moving. Feelings I had ceased to credit myself with were now profoundly stirred. Behind the large black cross, made out of charred wood, there had been carved in the stone the two simple words: ' Father, Forgive.' That was all and it was quite enough. If there is a nobler war memorial than this ruined cathedral, one that drives harder at that shell of chicanery, hypocrisy, or self-deceit in which we encase our hearts, I have yet to see it. Father, forgive! And outside in the streets they were selling the papers that told the same old story of indifference, drift, mischief, prejudice, passion, and blind idiocy."

Are not these two incidents deeply instructive and suggestive? In the one case a man gazes upon the cross but it awakens no answering response in his heart. He may already have been aware of the crosscurrents of human life, of the contraries of his own existence, of the naked tragedy of the world, of the *crucial* decisions (for so we call them) that he and his society were being forced to make. But the cross pattern of his life finds no interpretative key in the cross at which he looks. He knows nothing of the Man who suffered on a cross. He has never heard of God's forgiveness through a cross.

But the situation with Mr. Priestley is different. He is vividly aware of the tensions and conflicts and cross-purposes of his contemporary world. He knows the hypocrisy — the clash between the inward and the outward; the drift — the surrender to the backward; the passion — the descent to the downward; the contradiction between man as he is and man as he is meant to be. But when Mr. Priestley sees the charred cross and the carved words, there comes a sudden flash of illumination. Somehow the cross of Calvary *is* related to the cross pattern of human existence. Somehow the strange Man upon the cross speaking words of compassion and forbearance exposes the shams and follies of human life and yet in exposing them begins to heal them: man's destiny is not to be eternally at cross-purposes with himself, his world, and his God. Rather, through the One who was willingly stretched upon the cross, there have come the possibility and the hope of restoration, reconciliation, reintegration.

III

Here, then, is one of the major dilemmas of the Christian witness today. How can he bring together into meaningful relationship the cross in human life and the cross on the hill of Calvary, the cross in the experience of man and the cross in the experience of God? The task is so difficult that there has constantly been the temptation in Christian history to fall into one or other of two errors. Either the contrasting elements in these pairs are made to merge into one another completely or they are allowed to drift entirely apart.

In the first case, attention is focused upon the antagonisms and antitheses of the human situation in such a way that the suffering and death of Jesus seem to be nothing more than the most terrible illustration on record of the essential contradictions that belong to the ordinary human lot. The cross was a horrible instrument of torture. But was it altogether unrepresentative of the cruelty and the callousness that lurk beneath the surface wherever human societies are to be found? " To bind a Roman citizen," cries Cicero, " is an outrage; to scourge him a crime; it almost amounts to parricide to put him to death; how shall I describe crucifixion? No adequate word can be found to represent so execrable an enormity." That was the feeling of a sensitive man in Jesus' own time. But was crucifixion anything else than an extreme expression in that era of instincts and attitudes that are with us all the time?

This, which we may call the more *realistic* approach to the cross, whether in art or in poetry or in preaching, has concentrated attention upon its horrible and shameful features and has in effect declared: "*That* is the final demonstration of human sin and folly. *That* is the ultimate expression of human jealousies and contrarieties. *That* is the fate of the good man. *That* is the sign of the inner tragedy of all human existence." The cross on Calvary is thus in no essential way different from the cross within man's own experience. It only serves to expose once and for all the continuing inner realities of human nature.

But there is another approach to the cross. In this, attention is directed toward the glory and radiance that stream forth from the cross. It is, we are told, the supreme illustration of the divine capacity to remain untouched by the most savage designs of human cruelty. Did not the Son of God from the very beginning move majestically through the world, unaffected in his inner soul by the struggles and conflicts of his outward environment? Did not his divine serenity rise superior to all the passionate strivings of ordinary human nature? And did he not finally show himself impervious to the cruelties and devilish devices by which men sought to destroy his patient integrity? Thus the cross becomes transfigured.

> " O tree of beauty, tree most fair,
>   Ordained those holy limbs to bear,
>   Gone is thy shame, each crimsoned bough
>   Proclaims the King of glory now."

In other words the cross is the supreme illustration of the divine immunity to the most virulent diseases and infections that belong to the mortal scene.

This, which we may call the more *idealistic* approach to the cross, has concentrated attention upon its sublime and ethereal features and has in effect declared: " *That* is the final demonstration of the divine impassibility. *That* is the ultimate vindication of Life in the very charnel house of Death. *That* is the transcendence of all that is evil. *That* is the outward and visible sign that the inner life of God cannot be touched even by the darkest devices of sinful human nature." The cross on Calvary is thus utterly different from the cross within human existence. It is, in fact, the reversal of it, the denial of it, the recoil from it. It does not *interpret* the cross of man's experience but rather acts as a symbol of final separation from this earthly cross. It is decked with jewels, suffused with light, surrounded with emblems of glory and honor. The ordinary mundane cross remains uninterpreted; the imaginary heavenly cross dominates the scene.

We have set forth these two approaches in somewhat extreme form in order that we may be aware of these opposite dangers which have emerged in Christian history and are still with us today. To choose either one of these approaches and then to pursue it unrelentingly is to go along a path that gradually loses all meaning and ends either in despair or in unreality. Rather, the endeavor must constantly be made to hold in relationship with one another the cross in human experience and the cross in the divine purpose. And the place where these two are inextricably entwined together is within the wholeness of the career of Jesus Christ as set forth in the Gospels of the New Testament. We have spoken of a *fabric* of meaning. Nowhere can that fabric be seen in such perfection of form as in the life pattern of the Christ. Jesus Christ himself *evangelio suo vestitus* — clothed in his gospel — is the one toward whom our gaze must be directed as we seek to understand the meaning of human life in the light of the purpose of God.

In successive chapters, then, we shall consider the leading titles and descriptions that the New Testament applies to our Lord in connection with his saving work. As we seek to explore the implications of these titles the relation between the cross pattern of human life and the cross in His own life will perhaps become clearer. This does not mean that we can ever finally resolve the paradox of life through death, of victory through defeat, of justice through injustice, of glory through shame.

> " 'Tis mystery all! the Immortal dies!
> Who can explore His strange design?
> In vain the firstborn seraph tries
> To sound the depths of love divine;
> 'Tis mercy all! let earth adore:
> Let angel minds inquire no more."

So sang Charles Wesley in one of his finest Passion hymns, voicing the feelings of many as they approach the central symbol of the Christian faith. Yet it is not unrelieved mystery. As we trace the pattern of the story of the Son of Man we shall not walk in darkness but shall begin to enter into possession of the Light of Life.

> " O Lord, Christ, Lamb of God, Lord of Lords,
> call us, who are called to be saints,
> along the way of Thy cross:
> draw us, who would draw nearer our King
> to the foot of Thy cross:
> cleanse us, who are not worthy to approach,
> with the pardon of Thy cross:
> instruct us, the ignorant and blind,
> in the school of Thy cross:

arm us, for the battles of holiness
    by the might of Thy cross:
bring us, in the fellowship of Thy sufferings
    to the victory of Thy cross:
and seal us in the Kingdom of Thy glory
    among the servants of Thy cross,
        O crucified Lord;
who with the Father and the Holy Ghost
    livest and reignest one God
        almighty, eternal,
            world without end." Amen.

— *From* A Procession of Passion Prayers, *by E. Milner-White.*
S. P. C. K., 1950.

Chapter II

THE SAVIOUR–HERO

"Lo the Holy Hero-warrior King of glory.
He the Helm of Heaven hath arrayed the war
Right against his ancient foes, with his only might."

These are the opening lines of a poem that is considered to be the oldest Christiad in any modern European language. They bear striking witness to the fact that the human heart responds instinctively to a tale of struggle and conquest. The Christian philosopher may feel compelled to conclude that the Son of God was "inaccessible to any movement of feeling — either pleasure or pain," but the simple Christian believer recoils from such an idea. He is convinced that the story of Jesus' struggles and testings rings true and that nothing in the gospel is more heartening and inspiring than the record of the way he followed to enter into his glory. In our English versions of the New Testament, Jesus is not actually designated " Hero," but the ideas associated with the title correspond entirely to its central witness.

Perhaps the nearest parallel in the New Testament to the title we have chosen for this chapter is to be found in Acts 5:31. There Jesus is acclaimed as " Prince and Saviour " (King James Version) or "Leader and Savior" (Revised Standard Version). In the original the titles are coupled together so closely that a translation such as Hero-Saviour or Saviour-Hero would almost be possible. Jesus is the Hero in that he fully accepts the conditions of the human struggle — what we have called the cross of human existence — battles his way through the entrenched forces which oppose the carrying out of any spiritual purpose and wins through to a victory which changes the whole quality of human life and destiny. He is in truth a Pioneer, a Knight of the Cross, a Captain of Salvation (Heb. 2:10).

But Jesus is not to be regarded as a hero in the sense of one who engages in a conflict for conflict's sake, who stages, as it were, a demonstration battle, who enters with zest into the contest for its own excitement and satisfaction; he is a hero in the sense that his whole struggle is directed toward the achievement of a worthy end. He is the Captain who leads his followers to *salvation*. He is the Pioneer who through his own willingness to face danger and endure hardship opens the gates of new life to all who accept him as their Saviour and Guide.

It cannot be too strongly emphasized that this salvation of which the Bible speaks does not denote any kind of enclosed or walled-in state, any kind of security in which the possibilities of expansion no longer exist. The very name " Jesus " is derived from a Hebrew root that denotes " to be spacious." He is Jesus, Saviour, because he brings men out into a new spaciousness in every sense of the term. He breaks through the false securities and shams and compensatory oppressions of human life in order that he may lead his new race out into the place of light and growth and expansion and enlargement. " Salvation " means life at its highest level of experience. It means freedom from the cramping and confining limitations both of the world's prejudices and of our own timidities. The Hero-Saviour has won the decisive victory and thereby has brought near to man " the glorious liberty of the children of God." How this victory was accomplished we shall now examine in more detail.

TEMPTATION

The temptation story as it is recorded in Matt. 4:1–11 and in Luke 4:1–12 is one of the most profound and at the same time one of the most fascinating narratives to be found anywhere in the world's literature. Dostoevsky can scarcely restrain himself as he speaks of it. "If there has ever been on earth a real stupendous miracle," he writes, "it took place on that day, on the day of the three temptations. The statement of those three questions was itself the miracle. If it were possible to imagine simply for the sake of argument that those three questions of the dread spirit had perished utterly from the books and that we had to restore them and to invent them anew, and to do so had gathered together all the wise men of the earth — rulers, chief priests, learned men, philosophers, poets — and had set them the task to invent three questions, such as would not only fit the occasion but express in three words, three human phrases, the whole future history of the world and of humanity — dost Thou believe that all the wisdom of the earth united could have invented anything in depth and force equal to the three questions which were actually put to Thee then by the wise and mighty spirit in the wilderness? In those three questions the whole subsequent history of mankind is, as it were, brought together into one whole, and foretold, and in them are united all the unsolved historical contradictions of human nature."

It is hard to think that a narrative so concerned with the inner nature of Jesus' mission did not originate, at least in its essential outline, from the lips of Jesus himself. Some, indeed, prefer to think that it was the creation of some inspired writer of the Early Church. But whichever view is taken, there is general agreement that in the story of these temptations Jesus is depicted as being torn between two possible ways of fulfilling his vocation. Whether he was actually conscious of his Messiahship or not, he must have believed that he had some God-given task to fulfill. But how would he do it? What methods would he use? What tradition would he follow?

The first alluring possibility may be called "The Snare of the Short Cut." John A. Hutton has an instructive essay with this title in his book *The Dark Mile*. He recalls "how John Bunyan describes a road, called By-Path, which always had the look of being a shorter, simpler, more natural road . . . a road which indeed for a long time ran alongside the right road, which nevertheless after a night's journey had so diverged from the true road that you could not see the one from the other" (p. 102). How much shorter and simpler to turn stones into bread than to hear the Word of God and proclaim it! All men want bread: there is no guarantee that any man wants to hear the Word of God. How much easier to remove the harsh and rugged experiences out of men's way than to bear patiently with them in their bewilderment and distress! How many there are who love to follow the smooth and easy path: how few are ready to wait patiently upon God until he shows the way of life! Yet man only lives truly as he wrestles for the Word of God and then obeys it. Jesus rejected the short cut: he pioneered the way of faithful obedience to the Word of God and made it possible for men to follow him in the selfsame path.

The second possibility (following the Matthaean narrative) might be designated "Playing to the Gallery." This is the title of another essay in *The Dark Mile*. It is a natural desire to want to win the appreciation and even the approval of our fellow men. We are not made for solitude, and a task performed for oneself alone is a poor and unsatisfying thing. But in this desire for appreciation there lurks a deadly danger. It is possible to win the approval of those whose standards are low and unworthy by playing fast and loose with one's own inner integrity. It is possible to love the praise of men more than the praise of God. It is possible to create a sensation in the temple courts instead of renewing one's offering of devotion in the inner sanctuary. Jesus refused to purchase the plaudits of the crowd at the cost of toying with triviality. He would die rather than make a convenience or a cheap advertisement of the power and providence of God.

The third temptation may be entitled "Forcing the Issue." Gradually there took shape in Jesus' imagination the vision of a kingdom surpassing even the great Roman Empire of his day in the range of its inclusiveness and the efficiency of its organization. Could he not regiment the peoples of the world for their good? Could he not remove the possibilities of tensions and frictions? Could he not enforce order and strict discipline everywhere? Could he not employ the various devices by which men's minds can be numbed and their questionings stifled — slogans, propaganda, ideological dogmas? Could he not even regard it as his duty to remove men's obvious ills and to bring them into a condition of security and peace? But suddenly his whole soul recoiled from the prospect. It was the way of the deceiver. In pursuing it he would be yielding himself to the devil and not to God. The true God was a God of patience and long-suffering and mercy, a God seeking a willing love and not a blind servitude, a God concerned for men's growth in responsible freedom rather than for their efficient organization within a utopian society.

These ideas may seem so familiar to us today that we find it hard to realize how much Jesus played the part of pioneer and leader in struggling with these fundamental problems of human life. The short cut by the way of pandering to the lower appetites, the cheap success by the way of appealing to the baser emotions, the smooth revolution by the way of manipulating the less worthy motivations — these possibilities which are never absent from the human scene Jesus seriously contemplated and as decisively rejected. It is true that (in Luke's vivid words) the devil departed from him only for a season. In varied and subtle forms the temptations were constantly renewed. To simplify his task by performing miracles and signs, to turn aside from the pathway leading to anguish and suffering, to employ methods of force to compel men's obedience — again and again these possibilities were presented to him. The Gospels do not for a moment suggest that such temptations were too mundane or too trivial to be real to him. At the same time there is never the slightest indication that he faltered or failed in the heat of the struggle. He is the Hero who, in the words of a later writer, was in all points tempted like as we are yet without sin. So he is able to save to the uttermost all who are tempted — either to draw back or to rush ahead, either to fall below their ideals or to soar above the hard realities of daily life; he is able to save them in the sense of leading them forward to the place of fuller responsibility and perhaps more severe testing, the place nevertheless of a heightened consciousness of the call and blessing and sustaining energy of God himself.

SUFFERING

The writer of The Epistle to the Hebrews, to whom we have just referred, has a remarkable phrase in which he links temptation

with suffering: " In that he himself hath suffered being tempted."
Actually it can be translated in two ways. The essential meaning
may be that Jesus suffered in and by his temptations. " Their
fires were no scenic flames. Alternatives to what He believed was
the will of the Father had their word out, so to speak, in his consciousness. The issue is never represented as having been a fore-
gone conclusion — as if the alternatives only offered such an appeal as could be easily flicked away, or, as John of Damascus puts
it, ' dissipated like smoke.' He suffered, and the fierceness of the
struggle left its marks upon him " (A. B. Macaulay, *The Death
of Jesus,* pp. 133, 134). This interpretation is certainly a true one.
Yet the phrase may be translated equally to mean that Jesus was
tempted by his sufferings. Whether or not this was the meaning
that the author intended it may not be possible to decide, but at
least it may be claimed that such a thought is in harmony with
one of the main themes of the Epistle — that Jesus was made
" perfect through sufferings."

The connection between suffering and temptation has been im-
pressively worked out by A. B. Macaulay in the book from which
we have just quoted, and we shall follow the line of his exposition
in some further detail. He begins by pointing out that in all
circumstances suffering is not only " a state of physical or mental
pain " but at the same time " a condition which gives rise to temptations." Almost any kind of suffering that we can imagine comes
to man as a test of his character and his normal attitudes, testing
him not only to see whether he is able to endure but also to see
whether he can rise above the suffering and win a spiritual victory, even in the midst of the stress and the strain. In what
particular ways, then, are we to regard the sufferings of Jesus as
temptations? Macaulay suggests that there are two ways. In the
first place the sufferings " subjected him to a trial of his love for
men and of his faith in their redeemableness." From the beginning of his ministry he sought in every way to declare God's good
will to men. He consistently proclaimed good news of liberty and
healing and forgiveness. He labored without ceasing to bring men
to their true destiny within the Kingdom of God. But the end

result of it all was a chain of bitter events culminating in the mocking and scourging and nailing to the cross. Suffering within an atmosphere of sympathy and understanding is one thing; suffering within a context of hatred and callousness is quite another. Had the way of love entirely failed? Were men utterly past redemption? These were the temptations that must have assailed him often in his ministry but with concentrated intensity in the last hours of his earthly career. " But his love for men triumphed over their hatred of him, his faith in them over the worst they could do to him. . . . From this trial of his love and faith he emerged victorious, unembittered, without a semblance of sullenness or resentment in his heart: 'Father, forgive them; for they know not what they do'" (Macaulay, p. 136).

In the second place, Macaulay suggests, Jesus' sufferings " subjected him to a supreme trial of his filial relationship to the Father." Here already we reach what is in many ways the supreme mystery of the cross. Jesus has taken his place with sinful man. He has identified himself with man, in spite of man's pride and rebellion against God, in order to save him. But deep down in the tradition of the Jewish race lay the conviction that suffering is the consequence of wrongdoing, that distress of body and mind is at least part of God's judgment upon human folly. Could it then be that his own suffering was in some way related to his deliberate acceptance of solidarity with sinful man? Could it be that his agony was a mark of his being abandoned, that the face of God's holiness was necessarily averted from him as he numbered himself with the transgressors? Could such a cry as " My God, my God, why hast thou forsaken me " have been wrung from his lips unless some kind of bitter trial and testing had been going on in his innermost soul? Yet again it is impossible to think that he succumbed to this trial of suffering. There are later words from the cross that breathe a spirit of victorious confidence in God. Whatever his suffering means, it does not mean that God has abandoned him or even temporarily turned away from him. Never is the Son nearer to the Father's heart than in the hour of his bitterest trial; never is the Father nearer to the Son than in the moment of his deepest identification with those he had come to save.

Thus even in the midst of his suffering he is victorious. Christian art has tried to express this conviction through the paintings and crucifixes in which the Christ is depicted as strong in the midst of his weakness, as reigning in the midst of his ignominy, as victorious in the midst of his defeat. This does not mean that the Christ is untouched by his suffering so that he remains impassible and immutable through all that comes to him. Rather it means that he is the Hero who endures his suffering with indomitable fortitude, triumphs over all the attendant temptations that assail him, and thereby opens a door of salvation to all who suffer and to all who are tempted. "Though he were a Son, yet learned he obedience by the things which he suffered; and being made perfect, he became the author of eternal salvation unto all them that obey him."

Death

One of the most impressive passages in modern literature is to be found at the conclusion of Arnold Toynbee's discussion of the relations between disintegrating societies and individuals in the sixth volume of his *Study of History*. He points out that in a disintegrating society the creative individual is called upon to play the part of a savior. There are diverse types of would-be saviors and Toynbee considers these types in succession. There is the savior with the sword, the savior with the time machine — the leader, that is, who tries to find salvation either in an idealized past or in an idealized future — and the savior who seeks to remold society according to the pattern of his own philosophical system. All these are considered but rejected as having failed to bring the disintegrating society to salvation. Finally, Toynbee turns to the saviors who have presented themselves as gods. In particular he surveys the record of Hellenic mythology and the stories of the encounters of the gods with death. They are often noble, often beautiful. But how far short they fall of the story of the Son given by the Father in order that the world might not perish but have everlasting life!

" This is in truth the final result of our survey of saviors. When we set out on this quest, we found ourselves moving in the midst of a mighty host, but, as we have pressed forward, the marchers, company by company, have fallen out of the race. The first to fail were the swordsmen, the next the archaists and futurists, the next the philosophers, until only gods were left in the running. At the final ordeal of death, few, even of these would-be savior-gods, have dared to put their title to the test by plunging into the icy river. And now, as we stand and gaze with our eyes fixed upon the farther shore, a single figure rises from the flood and straightway fills the whole horizon. There is the Saviour; ' and the pleasure of the Lord shall prosper in his hand. He shall see of the travail of his soul, and shall be satisfied.' "

The encounter with death is the final test of the Saviour-Hero. Will he go forward steadfastly, courageously, unflinchingly? Death today may have lost some of its terrors. It may be regarded as a biological inevitability; it may be viewed as no more than a gateway leading to an unknown country. But men may hardly realize how much of this changed attitude is due to the influence of the Christian tradition with its proclamation of the Saviour's victory over death. Certainly in the world into which Christianity first came the fear of death was desperately real. In spite of centuries of enlightenment, the Greeks had never found release from this terror. The writer of The Epistle to the Hebrews knew the world of his day well enough and he describes men as being all their lifetime subject to bondage through fear of death. Yet the thrill of the New Testament is that One had been found who through death had overcome death and had opened to men the gate of everlasting life. " O death, where is thy sting? O grave, where is thy victory? . . . Thanks be to God, which giveth us the victory through our Lord Jesus Christ."

The theme of the Saviour's heroic encounter with and victory over death has been the inspiration of some of the most exultant and jubilant writing in Christian history. We might appeal to the early missionary bishop Irenaeus, who brought a message of hope, and victory to the Christians of southern Gaul. " He [Christ] has therefore in his work of recapitulation summed up all things, both waging war against our enemy, and crushing him who at the beginning had led us away captive in Adam in order that, as our species went down to death in a vanquished man so we may ascend to life again through a victorious one." Or we might turn to the pioneer Reformer, Martin Luther, who likewise brought words of encouragement to the German people of his day. Christ is the Lord, he says, who " has redeemed me from sin, from the devil, from death and all woe. For before, I had not yet had any Lord, nor King, but had been held captive under the devil's power, doomed to death, ensnared in sin and blindness. . . . Now, therefore, those tyrants and gaolers are all crushed, and in their place is come Jesus Christ, . . . and he has snatched us poor lost men from the jaws of hell, won us, made us free, and brought us back to the Father's goodness and grace."

But for evidence of the way in which the victory of Christ worked creatively in the imagination of peoples with no long heritage of culture behind them, we cannot do better than summarize the fascinating poem " The Dream of the Rood." Inscribed in runes on the Ruthwell cross, it bears witness to the spirit of Celtic Christianity in Northumbria in the seventh century. In the poem the " Saviour's tree " becomes alive and addresses the poet. It tells how it was hewn from the forest and set on a hill.

> " Then saw I mankind's Lord
> hastening in His might to ascend me there:
> I dared not then oppose the Word of God
> or bend or break asunder, though I saw
> earth's bosom quake; yea all His foes might I
> have laid full low, yet stood I firm.
> Then the young warrior prepared Himself —
> 'twas God almighty, resolute and strong;
> brave in the sight of many, He went up
> upon the lofty cross to save mankind."

Continuing, the tree tells how the " noble Prince " was slain, how the " Lord of Victory " was laid in a grave of bright stone,

and how the tree itself was felled to the earth and hid until its
hour of vindication and glory came.

> "Lo, me the Prince of Glory, Heaven's Lord,
>   hath glorified above all forest trees,
>   as He, Almighty God, hath glorified
>   His mother, Mary, above womankind."

Then the poem concludes with its paean of victory:

> "The Son came back as victor from the fight
>   with mighty triumph; with him a multitude,
>   a troop of souls, the mighty Sovran brought
>   unto God's kingdom. Joy to angels, joy
>   to all the saints then dwelling there in glory,
>   in Heaven's heights, when He, their ruler, came
>   the Lord Almighty, back into His realm."

Such a poem may contain legendary accretions and theological inexactitudes but it breathes the authentic spirit of the New
Testament. The Saviour-Hero has won the victory even over
death. He has conquered man's final enemy. He that was dead
is alive again and has the keys of hell and death. And he who
himself passed through the jaws of death and emerged victorious
on the farther side is able to save us from falling into despair and
to present us "faultless before the presence of his glory with ex-
ceeding joy."

In conclusion we may note that the writer of The Epistle to the
Hebrews focuses attention upon two aspects of death — the power
of death and the fear of death. As regards the first, he claims that
in some unspecified way the devil has the power of death. Death
would have no sting, no strangle hold, were it not for the fact
that the devil somehow uses it for his own purposes. Whatever
the author may have had in mind when making this statement,
may we not interpret it to mean that the devil can use death either
to crush men with a sense of frustration or to terrify them with a
sense of inexorability? It is sometimes the way of the spirit of
falsehood to tempt man to overreach himself (as in the Garden of

Eden) and then to dash his hopes to the ground by confronting him with the reality of his mortality. Or, tempting man first to settle complacently into a living death, he suddenly awakens him to terror by confronting him with the fact that real death threatens to bring his carefree lotus existence to an end. Thus he obscures the true nature of death and uses it as his instrument to deceive and subvert men to the very end. It is because of these twisted and distorted views of death that men are afraid of death. The cruel annihilation of their ambitions, the rude termination of their material comfort and ease, the final separation from the objects of their desires — these are the aspects under which death is seen and through which it gains its terrors.

But, says the writer of the Epistle, the Captain of Salvation through death destroyed him that had the power of death and delivered them who through fear of death were all their lifetime subject to bondage. Commenting on this verse, A. B. Davidson, in his book *The Epistle to the Hebrews,* writes:

" The Son came into the life of man that by going victoriously through it all he might altogether alter its complexion . . . In death his fellowship with God remained unbroken, and his supplication for salvation from death was heard for his godly fear. In him all the protests of Old Testament saints against death as separation from God and their aspirations for an overleaping of the condition of the dead became translated into history. But this history was not the history of an isolated individual but of the Leader of salvation. And through this history death assumed to ' every one ' who believed in him another aspect; it became part of a new order of things and the gate to that glory and honor to which the Son Himself had entered through it " (p. 70).

This is the overcoming of both the power of death and the fear of death — to see it under an altogether new aspect in the light of the career of the Captain of Salvation. Out of her richly varied experience of life the distinguished traveler and author Freya Stark writes in one place, " An absolute condition of all successful living whether for an individual or a nation is the acceptance of death." This may well be true. But surely it makes all the difference under what aspect it is accepted. " I am going to take a leap into the dark. I commit my body to the worms and my spirit to the great Perhaps." This is the acceptance of death by Hobbes the skeptic. " For to me to live is Christ, and to die is gain." This is the acceptance of death by Paul the Christian. In a certain sense each had gained his freedom from the fear of death. And yet it is the difference between the freedom of mere arbitrariness and uncertainty and the freedom of limitless expansion within a transcendent personal relationship. In the last resort it is for every man to choose the type of freedom within which he desires to live. But nothing can dim the fact that the Saviour-Hero accepted death— its power, its fear, its reality — and nothing can prevent the Christian from believing that *He* overcame. Wherefore " in all these things we are more than conquerors through him that loved us." In this sign we triumph. Through death we enter into everlasting life.

> " The royal banners forward go;
> The cross shines forth in mystic glow;
> Where He in flesh, our flesh who made,
> Our sentence bore, our ransom paid.

> . . . .

> " Fulfilled is all that David told
> In true prophetic song of old;
> Amidst the nations, God, saith he,
> Hath reigned and triumphed from the tree.

> . . . .

> " O cross, our one reliance, hail!
> So may Thy power with us avail
> To give new virtue to the saint,
> And pardon to the penitent.

> " To Thee, eternal Three in One,
> Let homage meet by all be done:
> Whom by the cross Thou dost restore,
> Preserve and govern evermore."
> —*Hymn translated from the Latin of Venantius Honorius*
> *Fortunatus* (A.D. 569). *Translated by J. M. Neale.*

CHAPTER III

THE GREAT SHEPHERD OF THE SHEEP

" But none of the ransomed ever knew
   How deep were the waters crossed;
Nor how dark was the night that the Lord passed thro'
   Ere He found His sheep that was lost."

In modern life the shepherd occupies a role of minor importance within the framework of human society. But looking back over the history of mankind, we discover that the shepherd has been a by no means insignificant figure. To shepherds have come determinative religious revelations; the character of the shepherd has provided the model for some of the noblest portraits of religious leadership. The shepherd's task may seem humble but it can be the channel through which unlimited devotion and self-sacrifice are outpoured.

At the dawn of Israel's history small communities of shepherds lived with their families and their flocks on the edge of the civilization of their day. The patriarchs are always described as tent dwellers and their pattern of life was that of the shepherd on the Syrian steppes. However far they allowed themselves to be molded to the pattern of Canaanite civilization, they could never forget that the life of the shepherd or the peasant was the true Israelitic life and many of the social ideals of the later prophets were drawn from the customs and sanctions of the earlier pastoral existence. It is surely not without significance that when Moses, the great hero of Israel, left the courts of Egypt and adopted the life of a nomadic shepherd, there came to him the revelation that was to influence his people's development more perhaps than any other single event in its history. It was the man who was faithfully discharging his duties as a shepherd in the loneliness and dangers of the wilderness who was chosen to be the leader and pastor of God's people in their emancipation from slavery and their establishment as an independent nation. Thus, in the true Israelite tradition, no higher calling than " shepherd " was recognized. No title more plainly revealed the character of their relation to their God than that which spoke of him as the Shepherd of Israel who led Joseph like a flock (Ps. 80:1).

But it was not only in the Israelite faith and tradition that the shepherd came to occupy a place of honor. Toynbee has pointed out that both in Hellenic mythology and in the record of the Christian evangelist shepherds " abiding in the field " were chosen to be the channels of new revelation. Why, he asks, are they " chosen out of all Mankind, to be the recipients of theogonies? " (*A Study of History,* VI, 363). No answer to this question can be more than speculative but Toynbee has one intriguing suggestion to offer. It is that when catastrophes overtake the centers of culture and sophistication, " the shepherds and herdsmen on the mountains survive " and in their guilelessness and simplicity prove to be ready transmitters of the new knowledge which is to take the place of the effete and outworn. At least we may say that the shepherd stands in the history of civilization as the type of the man who in the solitary places and in the midst of a life of rugged self-expenditure is alert to the voice from beyond and is quick to translate for the benefit of the market place the message which has rung in his ears in the silence of the desert.

Simple dignity, openness to revelation and nobility of character — this third characteristic has impressed watchers of more modern times. In an appealing passage John Buchan refers to the Scottish Border shepherds of his youth. He used to accompany them over the hills and into the market and to the places of dipping and shearing. " Those Border shepherds, the men of the long stride and the clear eye, were a great race — I have never known a greater . . . My old friends, by whose side I used to quarter the hills, are long ago at rest in moorland kirkyards and my salutation goes to them beyond the hills of death. I have never had better friends and I have striven to acquire some tincture of their philosophy of life, a creed at once mirthful and grave, stalwart and merciful." But coming even closer to our theme, in his famous

Historical Geography of the Holy Land, Sir George Adam Smith comments on the grandeur of the shepherd's character thus:

"I do not remember ever to have seen in the East a flock of sheep without a shepherd. In such a landscape as Judea, where a day's pasture is thinly scattered over an unfenced tract of country, covered with delusive paths, still frequented by wild beasts, and rolling off into the desert, the man and his character are indispensable. On some high moor, across which at night the hyenas howl, when you meet him, sleepless, farsighted, weather-beaten, armed, leaning on his staff, and looking out over his scattered sheep, every one of them on his heart, you understand . . . why Christ took him as the type of self-sacrifice." No human calling seemed to Jesus so adequate to represent his own vocation within the divine purpose as that of the shepherd. No more elevated title is applied to Jesus anywhere in the New Testament than that which we have made the title of this chapter: "The Great Shepherd of the Sheep."

Not only, however, is the appellation "shepherd" exceedingly appropriate to apply to those in history who have proved themselves to be leaders, media of revelation, saviors; the correlative term "sheep" has been all too appropriate to describe the generality of men, who have appeared to be harassed and scattered abroad as "sheep having no shepherd." In the days of Israel's sojourn in the wilderness, when Moses' period of leadership was drawing to a close, he appealed to God that he would "set a man over the congregation, . . . which may go in before them, and which may lead them out, and which bring them in; that the congregation of the Lord be not as sheep which have no shepherd" (Num. 27:16b, 17). In the days of the monarchy when bad leadership was bringing Israel to the brink of disaster, the prophet Micaiah, in a flash of vision, saw "all Israel scattered upon the hills, as sheep that have not a shepherd: and the Lord said, These have no master: let them return every man to his house in peace" (I Kings 22:17). When at length the Shepherd of the Lord appeared among men, his own heart was moved with compassion "because they fainted, and were scattered abroad, as sheep having no shepherd " (Matt. 9:36). Such is the plight of men in the eyes of the divine compassion — they are as sheep having no shepherd.

Or the matter is expressed in another way. Men have gone astray like lost sheep. In the famous words of Isa., ch. 53, all have gone astray, all have turned to their own way. In the poignant concluding words of the One Hundred and Nineteenth Psalm, an individual confesses that he has gone astray like a lost sheep: his only hope lies in the willingness of the divine Shepherd to seek the lost. The same picture is used by the writer of I Peter, quoting directly from Isa., ch. 53: " Ye were as sheep going astray; but are now returned unto the Shepherd and Bishop of your souls." Here is a picture of man not so much in his rebellion and perverseness as in his pathetic weakness and fecklessness. He has not deliberately planned to go astray. He has not wittingly turned his back on the green pastures. Rather he has kept his head down and followed his nose wherever it might lead him. He has taken no bearings; he has listened for no voice; he has simply been at the mercy of his appetites. So he finds himself lost, without direction, without hope.

Few of us who are honest will deny that this picture is extraordinarily apt to describe our own situation. We have gone astray like lost sheep. Herbert H. Farmer has written with penetrating insight: " The very fact that it has all come about in this lost-sheep kind of way makes the whole business seem so hopeless. A more or less conscious and deliberate turning on one side, serious as it is, seems a different matter: there is at least no mystery about it. There is something clear-cut and definite to repent of and to hold in the soul as a warning memory. But this straying business is so impalpable, so unintended, and yet so very definite in its result. Again and again in your journeying you lifted your eyes to the horizon and to the hills, again and again you tried to orientate your steps by the great landmarks of Christian faith and experience: nevertheless this is where you are, strayed into the flats of spiritual mediocrity and ineffectiveness." This is, then, the typical Biblical picture of the human predicament and it is against this background that the nature of the mission of the divine Shep-

herd can best be seen. We shall now seek to examine the task and
the achievement of the Shepherd in greater detail.

Unworthy Shepherds

Two types of unworthy shepherds are depicted in the Bible, and
these act as a foil to the characterization of the good and true
Shepherd. One type is the hireling whose picture is set before us
in John, ch. 10. "He that is a hireling, and not the shepherd,
whose own the sheep are not, seeth the wolf coming, and leaveth
the sheep, and fleeth; and the wolf catcheth them, and scattereth
the sheep. The hireling fleeth, because he is a hireling, and careth
not for the sheep." Obviously there is something reprehensible
about the hireling. He has no business to abandon the sheep to
the wolf: his attitude toward them is callous and irresponsible.
Yet there is something to be said on his behalf. He has not experienced the joy of ownership, with the sense of treasuring that
which belongs to him; strictly speaking, he has been hired to lead
the sheep to pasture, not to fight wild beasts. This hireling attitude
is one that has deeply infected modern life. Ever since the beginning of the industrial revolution, man in the Western world
has taken on the character of the hireling, possessing little of his
own, employed to perform a particular job, not responsible for
unexpected eventualities which may arise. He is not devoid of a
certain sense of responsibility for the machines or tools or products
or artifacts which he has to handle. But there is no warmth, no
passion, no real relationship, no readiness to go beyond that which
is written into the contract. He has no sense of obligation or of
ownership. Why should he care deeply or spend himself passion-
ately?

It is a significant fact that man cares deeply only for that which
he has begotten, that which he has created, or that which he owns
by purchase — the purchase representing his own outpoured
energy. The tragedy of the modern world is that the rapid growth
of population and the steady drain upon the earth's supply of raw
materials seem to imply that the possibilities of creative activity
or of satisfying ownership will tend to grow less and less. More-

over, the modern processes of mass production which seem to provide an abundance of things for those who desire to purchase them also seem to leave men strangely unsatisfied. There may be actual ownership but when the thing possessed is soulless, mechanical, completely uniform with thousands more and likely soon to be outdated by something better, it is hard to care for the thing with any intensity of feeling. The final result is that the family remains the only entity that draws forth any deep feelings of care and affection, and yet the family itself is not immune to the forces of disintegration which are at work in the wider world within which it is set. The family cannot be independent of its environment, and when the main forces operating in that environment are mechanical and impersonal and compulsive, it is next to impossible for an integrating spirit of mutual care to be sustained. Yet, if the hireling becomes the archetype of modern man and care perishes from the earth, all the tenderness and beauty will have gone out of life and the robot age will be at hand.

The second type of unworthy shepherd is that which is so vividly depicted in the thirty-fourth chapter of Ezekiel. Here is the shepherd who holds a position of responsible ownership but who proves himself utterly unfitted for his trust. He is not, like the hireling, the victim of his circumstances. Rather he is the man who deliberately uses his position of privileged ownership for his own individual gain. He feeds himself rather than the flock: he seizes the milk, he clothes himself with the wool, he kills the fatlings — in fact he simply exploits the flock for his own advantage. He is indifferent to the weak and the sickly, the cripples and the strayed. Let them go to the wall while he fattens himself on the rest! Obviously the policy is shortsighted, for a flock treated in such a way must quickly disintegrate and perish. But the false shepherd judges that the resources are sufficient to last out his own lifetime and he will exploit them to the limit.

The parallel to this attitude in modern man's exploitation of the earth's natural resources is too apparent to need emphasis. The soil, the water supply, the forests, the livestocks — all have been used without sufficient regard for conservation and renewal. Yet in more subtle ways man's attitude to his fellows or even to himself can all too easily become that of the false shepherds. All forms of oppressive imperialism, all attempts to exploit the forces of labor in industry, all schemes to milk a particular class or section of the community regardless of the consequences, all indifference to the needs of those of other races and colors — these all stand under the condemnation meted out to the false shepherds by Ezekiel. "Thus saith the Lord God; Behold, I am against the shepherds; and I will require my flock at their hand, and cause them to cease from feeding the flock; neither shall the shepherds feed themselves any more; for I will deliver my flock from their mouth, that they may not be meat for them." The judgment may be stayed and delayed but nothing is more certain, even within the records of human history, than that any individual or group that seeks to exploit another individual or group with greed and extortion is bound to reap that harvest of doom which the seeds of force and cruelty will produce.

It is almost impossible to leave the subject of "unworthy shepherds" without thinking of those who are set apart to the particular office of "pastor," those whose relationship to their fellows should be more truly comparable to that of a shepherd to his sheep than to any other human vocation. Few ministers are unaware of the temptations that beset them in their calling. Yet if ever a man begins to feel the least sense of complacency or self-satisfaction in his task, he will do well to measure himself afresh by the standards of John, ch. 10, and Ezek., ch. 34. Are the bonds that bind him to his people no stronger than those that connect the hireling to his temporary charges? Are they simply bonds of expediency and opportunism? Or is his relationship to them determined ultimately by the question of how it may turn to his own advantage, and serve either his vanity, his ambition, or his ease? How does he regard the diseased, the sick, the broken, the bewildered, the lost? A recent anthology of references to "the parson" or "the pastor" in English literature has revealed that in all too many cases he is depicted as a man enclosed in his own vanity or concerned for his own comfort. Again and again in

Christian history manifestations of anticlerical feeling have borne witness to a commonly held conviction that in some way the pastors were feeding themselves and not their flock, or that they were performing their duties mechanically as hired men rather than compassionately as shepherds to their own sheep. Rarely can such bitter words have been written as those which occur in William Langland's *The Vision of Piers the Plowman:*

> " I see examples myself, as may many another;
> Servants who serve lords seldom fall in arrears,
> As do the keepers of their lord's goods, clerks and stewards.
> The laity and the unlettered and men of little knowledge
> Seldom fall so far in arrears or so far in sinning
> As do clerks of Holy Church, who keep Christ's treasure,
> Or the store of souls for salvation, as God says in the gospel."
> — *From the translation of Henry Wells. Copyright Sheed & Ward, Inc., New York, 1935.*

Such is the record of unworthy shepherds. Let us turn from this to contemplate the picture of the altogether worthy — the Good Shepherd who gives his life for the sheep.

The Cost of Seeking

To seek the lost is always a costly business. This is true even in the most trivial experiences of human life. Once it is realized that an object that is valued for its own sake or needed for immediate use is lost, immediately there begins a process of attempted recollection, weighing of possibilities, experimenting in one direction or another, checking clues, seeking counsel, imploring aid. The more the object is valued, the greater the intensity of the search. A household tool, a domestic pet, a treasured symbol of personal relationship, a child of the family — it is possible to construct an ascending scale of values and everyone knows that there is no greater agony than that which the parent undergoes while the search is being made for the child who has disappeared. In any situation of this kind there is in fact the double costliness: that of the pain that comes of knowing that the treasured possession is lost, that of the travail of the actual search to retrieve the lost object from final destruction.

Possibly the most distinctive note of prophetic Judaism, in contrast to the emphases of other religious systems, is its constant proclamation that God himself seeks his erring children with an overwhelming intensity of longing whenever they go astray. In a certain sense, it is true that no man can ever wander beyond the confines of the knowledge of God. Yet when man withdraws from the sphere of active trust and obedience toward God and attempts to establish a realm of independent existence from which God is excluded, then to all intents and purposes he is lost from the household of God, he is wandering in alien country outside the Kingdom of righteousness and peace. Now it is altogether possible in such a case to adopt the attitude that whatsoever a man and a nation sow that must they also reap — and to wait for the processes of judgment to work themselves out. Much can be said in favor of such an attitude — it upholds the moral principles of the universe, it does not exonerate a man from his folly lightly, it seems true to an actual pattern that may be observed in human history. Yet the prophets of Israel, with all their insistence upon the righteous character of God and his just dealings with the sons of men, could not allow either that God stood by and let the processes of retribution work themselves out or that he limited his activities to the work of judgment in righteousness.

The gospel — for it was a real gospel — that they proclaimed was that God himself was ever searching for his sheep and seeking them out. Were they lost within the darkness of the bondage of Egypt? " I have surely seen the affliction of my people . . . and have heard their cry . . . ; I know their sorrows: and I am come down to deliver them out of the land of the Egyptians, and to bring them up out of that land." Had they forsaken the Lord God of their fathers and followed other gods? Nevertheless " the Lord raised . . . up judges . . . and delivered them out of the hand of their enemies all the days of the judge: for it repented the Lord because of their groanings by reason of them that oppressed them and vexed them." Had they sinned more and more and made them molten images of silver, and idols according to their own understanding? Had they made a covenant with the Assyrians and traded with the Egyptians? Yet the Lord drew them with cords of a man, with bands of love. "How shall I give thee up, Ephraim? how shall I deliver thee, Israel? . . . I will ransom them from the power of the grave; I will redeem them from death: O death, I will be thy plagues; O grave, I will be thy destruction." Had they been scattered in the cities of Babylon on a cloudy and dark day? "As a shepherd seeketh out his flock in the day that he is among his sheep that are scattered; so will I seek out my sheep. . . . And I will bring them out from the people, and gather them from the countries, and will bring them to their own land."

Such seeking, we may affirm, could never have been instituted and carried forward without cost. Yet the prophets hesitate to speak explicitly of a God who suffers. There are indeed pointers in this direction. We can hardly fail to catch the overtones of longing and anguish and compassion and distress as Israel's God considers the plight of his people. Why have they gone far away and followed after vanity? Why have they "forsaken me the fountain of living waters, and hewed them out cisterns, broken cisterns, that can hold no water?" Why have they been like animals running wild, heated with passion, out of control? Yet still let them only return, let them come back "and I will give you pastors according to mine heart, which shall feed you with knowledge and understanding." Again and again the cry rings out: "Return! Return unto me. There is no Saviour besides me. In me is thy help!" Nowhere is the agonized yearning in the heart of God more vividly portrayed than in the prophetic writings of the Old Testament.

But beyond this there is actual outward suffering in the lives of God's servants who bear witness to his backsliding people concerning their lost condition: "Which of the prophets have not your fathers persecuted? and they have slain them which showed before of the coming of the Just One." "O Jerusalem, Jerusalem, thou that killest the prophets, and stonest them which are sent unto thee." God was not indifferent to the sufferings of these his witnesses. Just as, in a later age, the man who persecuted the Christians was persecuting Christ himself, so in the earlier ages of Israel's history those who despised and rejected the prophets despised and rejected God himself. Yet the search went on, and so long as the true prophetic voice was heard, so long was there the witness to the costliness of the divine compassion.

Perhaps this prophetic witness was never altogether extinguished. In every age there are faithful souls who, having heard the call of the Shepherd themselves, join in the unending quest for the wandering and the lost. But allowing that this is so, the fact remains that in the late Judaism which immediately preceded the Christian Era, this particular witness was seldom heard. It is, indeed, difficult to speak with certainty about the thought and teaching of any special period in history; there may always have been humble groups of men proclaiming truths of which no outward record remains. Yet as far as our evidence goes, it seems that it was at this point more than anywhere else that the newness and originality of Jesus' mission and message were to be found. He proclaimed that it was God's will that the sinner should be sought out and reclaimed. Beyond this, he dedicated his own life to the task of seeking and saving that which was lost.

This matter is so interesting and so important that we shall dwell for a moment on the testimony of one of the noblest Jewish scholars of modern times. Time and again in his books, Claude Montefiore affirms that it was in Jesus' attitude to sinners that something altogether new appeared in the life of Judaism. " The virtues of repentance," he writes, " are gloriously praised in the Rabbinical literature, but this direct search for, and appeal to, the sinner are new and moving notes of high import and significance. The good shepherd who searches for the lost sheep, and reclaims it and rejoices over it, is a new figure, which has never ceased to play its great part in the moral and religious development of the world " (*The Synoptic Gospels,* II, 520–521). Or again: Jesus " sought to bring back into glad communion with God those whom sin, whether moral or ceremonial, had driven away. For him sinners [at least certain types of sinners] were the subject, not of condemnation and disdain, but of pity. *He did not avoid sinners but sought them out.* They were still children of God. This was a new and sublime contribution to the development of religion and morality . . . It is . . . a development of the best Old Testament teaching and it fits in with the Rabbinic teaching upon repentance. But to deny the greatness and originality of Jesus in this connection, to deny that he opened a new chapter in men's attitude towards sin and sinners, is, I think, to beat the head against a wall " (*The Synoptic Gospels*, I, 55).

These are striking words from the lips of a man who was intimately familar with the teaching of the rabbis of the early centuries of the Christian Era. There is, indeed, what Montefiore calls a " pretty " story in a Rabbinic commentary on Ex. 3:1: " While Moses was feeding the sheep of his father-in-law in the wilderness, a young kid ran away: Moses followed it until it reached a ravine, where it found a well to drink from. When Moses got up to it, he said, I did not know that you ran away because you were thirsty. Now you must be weary. He took the kid on his shoulders and carried it back. Then God said, Because you have shown pity in leading back one of a flock belonging to a man, you shall lead *my* flock, Israel." Such a story embodies a pretty fancy. But how different is the story of the man who left the ninety and nine and went after that which was lost — or, as the alternative record puts it, went into the mountains and sought that which had gone astray — until he found it! How different is Jesus' insistence that the very essence of his mission was to seek and to save that which was lost! There is no more revealing word in the Gospels than that which speaks of Jesus' being moved with compassion because he saw the people harassed and helpless like sheep having no shepherd. There is no more revealing phrase in the commission to the disciples than that which bids them go to the lost sheep of the house of Israel. The object of Jesus was to save and to redeem: " not to study, not even to teach those who chose to come and hear him within the synagogue or within the walls of the house of learning, but to go forth and actively seek out those who were in spiritual sickness or need, and to help and to cure them " (Montefiore, *op. cit.,* I, 29).

Such a mission, it almost goes without saying, could not be accomplished without cost. It has been argued that on the human level it was Jesus' attitude to sinners that was largely responsible for bringing him to the cross. It disturbed, it shamed, it infuriated the Pharisees. It constituted a contempt of the law that they could not forgive. Certainly such an identification with the fallen and the outcast could not have failed to arouse tension and anguish and longing in Jesus' own soul. A suggestion of the fate that awaited the shepherd of God's people is to be found in the quotation from the Old Testament recorded in Mark 14:27: " I will smite the shepherd, and the sheep shall be scattered." All these are only indirect indications of the costliness involved in the task of seeking for the strayed and the lost. But this at least is certain: He who prepares to seek the lost dare not neglect to count the cost. In the case of Jesus himself, had he been content to let well enough alone, to work out his destiny within the fold of conventional religion, how much pain and suffering could have been avoided! But his task was clear. He *must* seek the lost sheep. And the path to the mountains was the way of the cross.

The Cost of Caring

The distinction between the worthy and the unworthy shepherd has been expressed once for all in the tenth chapter of John's Gospel when it is said that the hireling has no *care* for the sheep. The good shepherd really *cares:* that is the mark that distinguishes him from all others who may in any way be related to the sheep. It is true that in Christian history the term " care " has been extended to describe a variety of functions included in the pastoral office, but originally and essentially it referred to an attitude of mind, a deep and intimate concern. One who cares for another takes the weight of the other's condition upon his own heart and bears it there steadily and unflinchingly. To use George Adam Smith's phrase already quoted, the shepherd who cares for his sheep bears them on his heart.

The word "care" has a long and interesting history. Although similar in form to the Latin words *cura* and *carus,* it appears to have no connection with either of them. In Old English it stands essentially for mental suffering, anguish, grief, which may be due to one's own individual sufferings. But gradually it came to be associated more with concern for others: a burdened state of mind brought about through fear of some danger that might be threatening a loved one, and so, ultimately, to any deep regard for another such as would cause one to spend and be spent on his behalf.

In the New Testament the earlier meaning still survives, though the later usage is fully established. "Be careful for nothing," "Casting all your care upon him" — these suggest the griefs and anxieties that weigh men down. "Take care of him," "He careth for you" — these suggest the deep concern and readiness for sacrifice which one feels toward another. One of the most striking appearances of the word in the New Testament is near the conclusion of Paul's attempt to vindicate his own apostleship on the ground of all that he had suffered and endured in the fulfillment of his vocation. Beaten, stoned, shipwrecked, in constant peril, "in weariness and painfulness, in watchings often, in hunger and thirst, in fastings often, in cold and nakedness. Beside those things that are without, that which cometh upon me daily, the care of all the churches. Who is weak, and I am not weak? who is offended, and I burn not?" This was the heaviest burden which Paul carried, this was the source of his intensest suffering. He felt for his converts, he suffered with them, he feared for them, he was indignant on their behalf, he hoped for them, he endured for them. No outward afflictions troubled him in the way that the trials and temptations of his converts did. He filled up that which remained of the sufferings of Christ in his flesh for the sake of the Body, that is to say, the Church (Col. 1:24). If any follower of Christ knew the costliness of caring, it was Paul.

But this attitude in Paul, as he would have been the first to admit, did not originate from any general feeling of good will or interest that he possessed in his own nature. His suffering was a part of the completion of Christ's sufferings; his care was a reflection of Christ's care; his sacrifice was a continuation of Christ's sacrifice. For it was only in Christ that the pattern of true care had been once for all revealed and it was only in fellowship with him that the burden of the world's guilt and anxiety could be borne at all.

So we return to the allegory of John, ch. 10. " The hireling . . . careth not for the sheep. . . . The good shepherd giveth his life for the sheep." He knows the sheep one by one, he recognizes the dangers to which each is exposed, he longs to lead each into the experience of richer and more abundant life. In other words, he *cares*. And because he cares, he is ready even to lay down his life for the sheep. But the question still remains: If he is willing, is that not enough? Was it necessary for Jesus to go to the limit of actual death when already it was clear that he had taken the sheep upon his shoulders and upon his heart and was making them to lie down in green pastures and was leading them beside the still waters?

To this question two answers may be tentatively given. The first is that because the forces of evil in the world are bitterly and consistently opposed to every attempt to lead men into the ways of pleasantness and peace, it was inevitable that the one who beyond all others adopted the shepherd role and began to be the Saviour of his people should have been the target of the most vicious attack ever launched by the powers of darkness. In the world of today, as all may see, any proposal to make possible a more abundant life for a wider circle of men immediately arouses the forces of reaction which have entrenched themselves behind walls of complacency and indifference. Much more in the world to which the Christ came, his proposal to give abundant life not only to the lost sheep of the house of Israel, but also to those " other sheep " who had never heard the voice of God — such a proposal was bound to bring the wolves howling around him and to lead ultimately to his death.

The second answer is that only through the actual public sight of the Shepherd crucified could the sheep forever know how much he cared. His words might reveal something of his care; his patient understanding and sympathy might reveal more. But when men had seen Jesus Christ in his death openly placarded before their eyes (Gal. 3:1), when they had beheld the Lamb led to the slaughter and lifted up upon the cross to die, then they knew that God cared and that nothing could separate them from his love. As George Orwell has so brilliantly shown in his novel *Nineteen Eighty-four,* once a man has reached the stage of caring only for himself — sacrificing even the one he had loved most to his own advantage — then he has ceased to be man. On the other side we may say that once a man has reached the stage of caring absolutely for another — even to the point of sacrificing his own self for the other's advantage — then he has begun to partake of the likeness of God. " Greater love hath no man than this, that a man lay down his life for his friends. Ye are my friends, if ye do whatsoever I command you."

" O merciful God, who hast made all men, and hatest nothing that thou hast made, nor desirest the death of a sinner, but rather that he should be converted and live; Have mercy upon all who know thee not as thou art revealed in the Gospel of thy Son. Take from them all ignorance, hardness of heart, and contempt of thy Word; and so fetch them home, blessed Lord, to thy fold, that they may be made one flock under one shepherd, Jesus Christ our Lord, who liveth and reigneth with thee and the Holy Spirit, one God, world without end. Amen." — *Collect for Good Friday,* The Book of Common Prayer.

CHAPTER IV

THE SON WHO WAS NOT SPARED

"Thou didst not spare Thine only Son,
But gavest Him for a world undone,
And freely with that blessed One
Thou givest all."

Is there any place in the literature of the English-speaking peoples where deep pathos and firm restraint are more exquisitely combined than in the parable of the Tenants in the Vineyard (Mark 12:1–8)? The parable begins in a matter-of-fact way, telling of the preparation of the vineyard, the arrangements for the lease, and the departure of the owner into a far country. It continues with a perfectly natural statement about the sending of the owner's representative to collect the agreed rent — when suddenly the whole scene changes as the tenants, for no apparent reason, maltreat the emissary and send him away empty. From this point in the story the dramatic tension grows, though on the surface the language remains severely simple and unadorned. Servant after servant comes but the treatment meted out to each becomes ever more barbarous. Then at length we reach the climax. The words are uttered quietly and simply but what a depth of feeling lies behind them, what an infinite range of suggestiveness!

"Having yet therefore one son, his well-beloved, he sent him also last unto them, saying, They will reverence my son."

Was the vineyard or were the tenants really worth the sending of the only son, the well-beloved? Was there any real likelihood that the attitude of the tenants would change? The answers to these questions are scarcely in doubt. Yet the lord of the vineyard made the final gesture of trust and hopefulness. How could they fail to honor the son? But the final gracious action of the owner only served to expose the inner feelings and motives of the tenants. "Come, let us kill him, and the inheritance shall be ours!" Lust for possession and power murders the rightful heir. The son who was not spared tastes the last dregs of the cup of human infamy and shame.

As one reads this deeply moving story, a contrast springs to mind from one of the most beautiful stories of the Old Testament. The prophet Nathan, desiring to bring home to the king the real nature of his acts toward Uriah and his wife, frames a simple parable in which one of the principals is an exceedingly wealthy man who possesses all that heart could wish. Over against him is set the poor man whose only possession is one ewe lamb. But when through the arrival of a guest an animal is needed for the feast, the rich man " spared to take of his own flock and of his own herd, . . . but took the poor man's lamb, and dressed it for the man that was come to him." To compare these two stories is to gain a degree of insight into the very essence of the contrast between man's sin and God's grace. Man spared to take of his own; God spared not his own son. Man robs his fellow even of his single ewe lamb; God, with his son, freely gives us all things. On the one side the depth of human meanness; on the other side the majesty of God's love!

The actual phrase, " He that spared not his own Son " occurs at the mid-point of one of Paul's most lyrical passages. He has no illusions about " the sufferings of this present time "; he hears the groaning of the whole creation as well as the anguished cries of human hearts; he recognizes that God's people are to all outward appearances like sheep being prepared for the slaughter. Yet, he cries — and this is the turning point of the passage, " If God be for us, who can be against us? " " He that spared not his own Son, but delivered him up for us all, how shall he not with him also freely give us all things? " Does man need justification, vindication, encouragement, confidence, hope? All these and more are contained in the gift of God's Son. A God who spared not his own Son can be trusted through time and eternity, for nothing can separate us from the love of God which is in Christ Jesus our Lord.

Sonship and Suffering

Surely one of the most daring statements in the New Testament is that found in Heb. 5:8: " Though he were a Son, yet learned he obedience by the things which he suffered." That the Son of God's love should need to learn anything seems strange; that he should need to learn obedience seems stranger; that he should learn it through suffering seems strangest of all. To understand the force of this statement, we shall need to see it within the wider context of the whole book.

The Epistle to the Hebrews begins with the majestic pronouncement that God, who had spoken unto the fathers of old through many prophets, had at one critical period of history spoken to their children in and through his Son. This Son was no ordinary human being. Through him God created the worlds, through him God still speaks to man, through him God will bring the whole created order to its proper fulfillment. He is the outward expression of the inner divine nature. He is the inward sustaining principle of the whole universe. He is the power of redemption at work in human life. Because he is the Son of God, he holds a position of dignity high above all other created beings. He is destined ultimately to have all things in subjection under his feet.

On this high note the writer begins his Epistle. He leaves us in no doubt about the uniqueness of the Son in the whole economy of things. He makes it altogether plain that Jesus is entitled to the name " Son " in a way that no other created being is. He affirms in so many words that the Son is the beginning and the end of all things, the same yesterday, today, and forever. Yet in the middle of the second chapter he strikes a new and unexpected note. It is the note of suffering, even the note of death. This exalted Son, holding these high prerogatives, has yet, for some reason, entered into the experience of suffering and death. Small wonder that to many in the Hellenistic world of the writer's own day this must have seemed incongruous, inconsistent, and even incredible. Why should it have been necessary for the heir of all things to endure real suffering and to taste the reality of death? Why could he not have been spared such agony and shame?

It is the task of the writer — a task that he triumphantly accomplishes — to bring meaning out of this seeming contradiction. To do this he appeals to two fundamental principles:

1. That one who would save others must himself be identified with them in every possible way.

2. That one who would restore his fellows to a position of full obedience to God must himself know what perfect obedience means from within the human situation. Let us examine each of these principles with some care.

First, the need for a complete identification is revealed through certain vivid and unforgettable phrases. Jesus is referred to as the Pioneer — the man, that is, who shares his people's lot and leads them toward their proper goal. He is depicted as the brother or father who has adopted his people into this particular relationship to himself. He has made them his brethren or his children. And to do this he has clothed himself with flesh and blood, he has shared their sufferings, he has tasted their death. Or, to put it in still another way, he has made himself their priestly representative, feeling with them the strain of their infirmities and weaknesses, tested like them by the afflictions that all men have to endure and finally offering on their behalf that sacrifice which is expected of them but which they have been unable to provide. In these various ways the author establishes his fundamental contention that Jesus, the Son of God, identified himself in every respect with those he came to save. Had any part of the human lot been excluded from the process of identification, that part would thereby have remained outside the possibility of purification and sanctification.

In the second place the writer fastens upon the virtue of obedience as being the hallmark of a true child of God and shows that Jesus himself, having learned a full-orbed obedience within the human situation, is able to lead others into that same obedient relationship which he experienced himself. Behind this emphasis on obedience there may well lie the tacit recognition that the original sin of man was *disobedience*. Here was man's most vulnerable point — the desire to take his own way rather than God's. And it was here that the Second Adam had to be tested in his assumed humanity. Would he also submit to the temptation to take his own way or would he remain faithful to the will of God all his journey through? The writer's triumphant assertion is that Jesus learned obedience in all its completeness through the things that he suffered, and thereby became the agent of an eternal salvation for all who learn to obey him.

" Though he were a Son, yet learned he obedience " is such a remarkable phrase that we shall quote a great commentator's interpretation of its meaning. " It is not remarkable," writes Dr. A. B. Davidson, " that a son should be obedient and it is not meant that the disposition of obedience was ever wanting to him. But the disposition had to maintain itself in the face of greater and greater demands upon it. And as he had to meet these demands rising with the rising tide of things which he suffered, he entered ever more deeply into the experience of what obedience was. For the demands could not be met without the resistance and shrinking of his human nature and the overcoming of this was an advance in obedience " (Heb. 3:2). The final stage in the learning of obedience was the acceptance of the cross. The keynote of Jesus' life had been, " Lo, I come to do thy will, O God," and at the end he willingly offered his body to the sacrifice of the cross, thus consummating a career of perfect obedience and opening a door of sanctification to all who enter into the obedience of Christ himself. " The obedience of the believer to Christ answers to the obedience of the Son to the Father. By obedience fellowship is made complete " (Westcott, *The Epistle to the Hebrews,* p. 129).

Thus the Son of God, the Heir of all things, the Lord of all the ages, identified himself with mankind in every respect save that of being ready to sin. He rejected the way of self-advancement through disobedience to God and passed instead through an experience of obedience which steadily widened in its range. Finally, by surrendering himself to death, he completed his obedience, for no greater sacrifice can be asked of anyone than that he should yield up his body to death. The life of perfect sonship within the eternal being of God has been once for all expressed under the conditions of human life. The way of obedience is now open to all who will follow him in the same willingness to learn through suffering.

GETHSEMANE

So far we have spoken in general terms of the process of learning obedience through the experience of suffering. But in the section of The Epistle to the Hebrews to which we have referred, one particular form of the Son's experience is singled out for special mention. It is his prayer life in the days of his flesh with its consummation in the agony of the Garden of Gethsemane. Let us set out the author's statement in the form in which it is found in the original:

> " In his days of flesh,
> having offered up,
> with strong crying and tears,
> prayers and supplications
> unto him that was able to save
> him out of death,
> and having been heard
> for his godly fear,
> though he was Son, yet learned
> obedience by the things which he suffered."

There is general agreement that there is here no exclusive reference to Gethsemane. It was through a lifetime of prayer that a full obedience was gradually fashioned. At the same time the close parallels to the Gospel accounts of the scene in the Garden make it almost certain that this experience was in the forefront of the writer's mind.

This picture of the prayer life of the incarnate Son is an exceedingly striking one. There is little suggestion of " mystic, sweet communion " or of " peace, perfect peace." In the phrase " prayers and supplications," " the first word," writes Westcott, " is the general term for a definite request. The second describes the supplication of one in need of protection or help in some over-whelming calamity. The one is expressed completely in words; the other suggests the posture and external form and emblems of entreaty " (p. 125). This phrase, then, brings to view a man in deadly earnest, expressing his concern in urgent speech and match-ing his speech with appealing gestures of the whole body. " Hav-ing offered up . . . unto Him that was able to save " further sug-gests the taking of each strong desire that arose in his heart and the definite offering of it Godward, offering it in sacrifice, offer-ing it in the context of a readiness to do the will of his Father at whatever cost. One other phrase may be regarded as representing the quality of all his prayers: it is " for his godly fear." The Greek word translated " godly fear " is an interesting one. It " marks that careful and watchful reverence which pays regard to every circumstance in that with which it has to deal. It may therefore degenerate into a timid and unworthy anxiety; but more com-monly it expresses reverent and thoughtful shrinking from over-boldness, which is compatible with true courage " (Westcott, p. 127). A careful presentation of his case coupled with a reverent willingness to accept the Father's will — such, it would seem, is the force of the word in this context.

But now there are two phrases that can hardly fail to recall Gethsemane: " With strong crying and tears "; " Him that was able to save him out of death." The first phrase reveals the in-tensity of the feeling contained in prayer at its highest. Westcott aptly quotes a Jewish saying to the effect that " there are three kinds of prayers each loftier than the preceding: prayer, crying, and tears. Prayer is made in silence; crying with raised voice; but there is no door through which tears do not pass." The prayer of Jesus in Gethsemane was such that it rose to a poignant cry and beyond that to sweat, " as it were great drops of blood falling down to the ground." In crying and sweat and tears his prayer rose to " Him that was able to save him out of death." Does this mean " Him that was able to save him from the necessity of undergoing death " or " Him that was able to save him, out of the actual experience of death, into newness of life "? Possibly the author had both in mind, but there can be little doubt that, as applied to Jesus, the first must be kept primarily in view. He prayed that if God were willing the cup might pass from him: " Nevertheless, not my will, but thine, be done."

Such is the description of Jesus' prayer life as given by The Epistle to the Hebrews. To supplement this account we shall turn to the Gospel accounts of the agony in the Garden. In these the central and altogether determinative symbol is "the cup." " Let this cup pass from me." " Take away this cup from me." " Father, if thou be willing, remove this cup from me." What is this cup that occupies so central a place in Jesus' thoughts? He had once asked two of his disciples whether they were able to share his cup. Now he holds the cup in his own hands and dreads to drain it to its depths. What is this cup?

It can scarcely be doubted that, as in the case of so many other language symbols that appear in Jesus' sayings, so here, the Old Testament must be regarded as the primary source. In The Psalms we find references to a cup of festive joy: " The Lord is the portion of mine inheritance and of my cup." " Thou anointest my head with oil; my cup runneth over." But in other psalms and in the writings of the prophets the cup is also a cup of judgment, of suffering, of bitterness. " God is the judge: he putteth down one, and setteth up another. For in the hand of the Lord there is a cup, and the wine is red; it is full of mixture; and he poureth out of the same: but the dregs thereof, all the wicked of the earth shall wring them out, and drink them." " O Jerusalem, which hast drunk at the hand of the Lord the cup of his fury; thou hast drunken the dregs of the cup of trembling, and wrung them out." And in Ezek., ch. 23, one of the most terrible chapters of judgment in the Old Testament, Jerusalem is told that the cup of her sister Samaria will be delivered into her hand. " Thus saith the Lord God; Thou shalt drink of thy sister's cup deep and large: thou shalt be laughed to scorn and had in derision; it containeth much. . . . Thou shalt even drink it and suck it out."

In the light of these passages it seems clear that the cup that Jesus held in his hands in the Garden was in some way related to the cup of the divine judgment upon the accumulated sin of his fellow men. Through the days of his flesh he had known stubborn opposition and deliberate misrepresentation. Pride and prejudice, envy and hypocrisy, had conspired to resist his work. Now the treachery of Judas, the instability of the disciples, the fickleness of the multitudes, were already pressing in upon his soul. The cup already contained much and would contain more. The drinking of the cup could not fail to involve suffering. Could he drink that cup? Could he take it out of the hands of those whose follies had caused it to be mixed and drain it to its depth? " Abba, Father, if it be possible, let this cup pass from me "!

No one dare speak with confidence as he seeks to interpret the meaning of the cup, the crying and the tears. On the one side there is clearly an agonized shrinking; on the other side, equally clearly, there is an instinctive trust in the One known by the tender name " Abba, Father." How can the two be reconciled? This will ever be a problem for interpreters and all must speak with restraint. Let us listen to two. " What the agony in Gethsemane reveals," writes Bede Frost, " is not a conflict between the divine and human wills in the One Person of the Word-made-flesh, for such a conflict constitutes the essence of sin, but a tension between the sensitive, lower part of the human soul of Jesus, seat of the passions and emotions, and the higher, rational and willing part. The distinction is known by every man who, in some time of crisis or danger, has shrunk with a natural, sensible repugnance and fear from the evil which threatened him whilst at the same time he has steadfastly resolved to endure it rather than lose his integrity, or to sacrifice the end which he had set before him." Apart from the questionable distinction between the " higher " and the " lower " parts of the soul of Jesus, this comment is suggestive and helpful. We can understand something at least of the tension involved when the purpose of a lifetime seems to be threatened by the inescapable challenge of the moment.

Our second interpreter is a theologian of an earlier generation. In his famous discourse delivered before the Harvard Divinity School more than a century ago, Horace Bushnell asks what account may be given of this "wonderful and peculiar passage" in the history of Christ. It was from no human fear that he was suffering; nor was it from any sense of the withdrawal of the Father's presence. Why then " is he wrenched by this so peculiar agony?" " Consider, I answer, that in the outward humanity of Jesus there is held, in some close and mysterious union, a divine nature; and then will our physiologists or physicians tell us how long a vehicle so slender is to support the tremendous reaction of compassions and struggles of feeling that are so deeply toned! Or, when the vehicle breaks under the burden, by what pathological signs it will be discharged! . . . Now, that which is itself the type and fruit of sin, bodily death, is at hand to be experienced. Will any psychologist or theologian tell us exactly how he ought to feel, whether he will suffer less than a man, or more? If innocence shudders at the thought of wrong, more than a soul that is dulled and half disintegrated by the consciousness of wrong, may it not, for the same reasons, shudder with a more intense horror before the prospect of that complete disintegration or tearing asunder which is the natural doom of wrong? If, too, a massive engine may shake, or even sink, a frail and poorly timbered vessel; or if a gigantic, masculine soul, knit to the body of a feeble and delicate woman, and, in that, called to suffer martyrdom, might possibly cause it to shudder and shake with a more insupportable horror than the delicate, feminine soul appropriate to its measure would do, what kind of demonstration shall be expected, when the Incarnate Word is summoned to die? I only inquire, you observe — I assert nothing for the very sufficient reason that I know nothing. Enough for me that my Redeemer, my most painstaking Saviour, falters not. Enough for me, that in that bloody sweat, falling on the desecrated earth, I see the love God has for love, the unspeakable desire he feels to win us back from sin, to re-establish the order of his realm, and hallow, for eternity, in our hearts, the sanctity of his violated law." Some of Bushnell's ideas may seem strange to us today, but there is no escaping the depth of feeling and sympathy contained in his words. At least he does full justice to the two elements which every valid interpretation must take into account — the obvious horror with which Jesus regarded the cup as well as the noble spirit of trusting obedience which animated him throughout the experience. Between these two elements there was an almost unendurable tension and strain. All of which suggests that it was in Jesus' prayer life that his sufferings were mostly deeply felt. This thought we shall seek to explore more fully.

THE ATONEMENT AS PRAYER

One of the most striking changes in thought about the atonement during the past century has been the shift in emphasis from the consideration of Jesus' sufferings as endured outwardly in the body to the contemplation of his struggles as carried on inwardly in the soul. In saying this we do not intend to set up too sharp a distinction between body and mind or to suggest that bodily suffering and mental suffering are independent of one another. But for centuries in Western Christendom the agony of Jesus was portrayed either through the realism of paintings and sculptures or through language which compared his sufferings to those that criminals endure when the justice of the law inflicts upon them their due punishment and reward. Doubtless there must also have been mental suffering but this aspect of things did not receive such careful analysis. Either men gazed upon some vivid picture of the crucifixion and reacted instinctively to the sight of the suffering Christ, or in a more detached manner they set the sufferings within a framework of the processes of penal justice and recognized that such an acceptance of punishment was necessary in order that the law might be upheld and the debt of sinners paid.

A little over a century ago, however, a new approach to the sufferings of Christ began to be made. Could it be that too much attention had been paid to the physical sufferings and not enough to the mental anguish? Had Christ in his sufferings been regarded too much from the *human* side, that is, as enduring as man for man the last penalty of sin? Had there been too much emphasis upon the majestic *law* of God and not enough upon the unlimited *love* of God? Might it not be that the sufferings of Christ were not so much inflicted by God as sympathetically shared by God? At least might it not be possible by exploring more deeply the nature of the relationship between the Father and the Son — assuming that Jesus was indeed the well-beloved Son — to see the atonement as being worked out within that relationship and therefore as being dependent upon movements of the imagination and consciousness which are only dimly expressed in outward physical ways?

With this shift of emphasis the focus of attention became not so much the final events of the judgment hall and Golgotha as the significant inner experiences of Jesus' life of which the record has been preserved — the temptation, the transfiguration, Gethsemane. The center of examination became not so much the legal metaphors of the Pauline writings as the Gospel records of Jesus' own words, describing his mission within the divine purpose. If his life and death were all of one piece, then it was of the highest importance to search for my clues which his own sayings might provide toward the meaning of the reconciliation which he was effecting. And it could be assumed that nowhere were clues more likely to be found than in his own inner experiences of prayer, when the Father was making his will known and when Jesus on his part was laying his inner consciousness open to God. In a very real sense Jesus' prayer life could be regarded as the central place of atonement. Calvary was the outward and visible sign of suffering and triumph already achieved in the inner life of wrestling in prayer.

In the development of this line of thought during the past century Christian theologians have tended to follow one or other of the following paths of interpretation. Some have taken the concept of sacrifice as self-offering and have seen in the prayer of Christ the pattern of all self-offering to God in the spirit. We shall return to this most important and fruitful idea in a subsequent chapter. Others have taken the concepts of confession and intercession and have seen in the prayer of Christ the supreme example of vicarious atoning activity within the whole realm of the relations between God and man. Perhaps the pioneer in this type of thinking was the saintly Scottish minister John McLeod Campbell, a man ejected from the Church of his own day because of teachings that seemed to be heretical, but since vindicated and acclaimed as one of the profoundest of all interpreters of the meaning of the death of Christ.

Campbell's basic presupposition is that God (whom he loves to designate " the Father of our spirits ") desires above all things that men may walk before him as dear children, and thereby attain their true destiny. He saw around him in his own day many who were content to admire God in his works of creation and even to use gratefully the universe which he had made but who never went beyond this to experience the life of sonship and trust and communion which is consummated in prayer. It was because men were content so to live that the Son of God came forth, revealing God as the Father and living within humanity the life of perfect sonship. For " we see the Father when we see the Son, not merely because of identity of will and character in the Father and the Son, but *because a father as such is known only in his relation to his son.*" The phrase that I have italicized becomes for Campbell the key to unlock the whole mystery of the atonement. It is in prayer that the relation between father and son is most perfectly revealed. Therefore the prayer experience of Jesus is the heart of the atonement and it is by reverent inquiry about the nature of that experience that we shall come nearest to the heart of the mystery itself.

In Campbell's analysis of the relation between the Father and the Son, there is no suggestion that it could be a relationship of the alone with the Alone. It is axiomatic for him that the one who loved his Father with all his heart and mind and strength loved his brethren as himself. " He, the perfect elder brother, unlike the elder brother in the parable, sympathized in all the yearnings of the Father's heart over his prodigal brethren; and the love which in the Father desired to be able to say of each of them, My son was dead, and is alive again; he was lost and is found, in him equally desired to be able to say, My brother was dead, and is alive again; he was lost, and is found." How, then, could the Son, sharing the Father's yearning and at the same time sharing the brethren's lot, act in such a way as to bring his brethren into the enjoyment of that relationship which was the very life of his own life?

Speaking in the simplest terms, we may say that Campbell had realized afresh that the most wonderful thing known to us in human life is for one person to take another's burdens on his own heart and carry them into the presence of God. If the burden is a burden of sin, then suffering is bound to be involved, for he cannot fail to see the sin in the light of God's standard of holy judgment, while at the same time his whole heart is set toward the establishing of a condition in which his brother can live as a free son in the family of God. Campbell receives a flood of light on his problem as he contemplates the incident recorded in Num. 25: 10–13. When a plague of judgment was raging in the camp of the Children of Israel, one man, Phinehas, stayed the plague by performing an act which at first sight seemed impetuous and arbitrary. But the important thing, says Campbell, was " the moral element in the transaction — the mind of Phinehas, his zeal for God, his sympathy in God's judgment on sin — this was the atonement, this its essence." In other words to share the mind of God toward sin and at the same time to enter into his yearning toward the sinner, that is the essence of atonement, and it is something that can be experienced in the inward life of prayer even more than in the outward circumstances of historical event.

We come now to the central portion of Campbell's book. Here we find him developing his theme under four headings. In its retrospective aspect the atonement reveals Christ, first, as dealing with men on the part of God and, secondly, as dealing with God on behalf of men. In its prospective aspect exactly the same is true. Taking first the retrospective aspect, which is concerned with man's guilty past, we see Jesus perfectly trusting the will of the Father against which man was rebelling, perfectly loving the brethren who were unworthy of the name of sons. In his prayers he committed himself again and again to that good and acceptable and perfect will of God; at the same time he entered into the suffering which God himself feels because men refuse to put their confidence in him. This was the witness to men on behalf of God. Further, however, he witnessed to God on behalf of men by making a perfect confession of our sins and by accepting to the full God's judgment upon them. Such a confession, says Campbell, was " a perfect Amen in humanity to the judgment of God on the sin of man." He bore the burden of our sins into the holy presence of God, and receiving the full impact of the divine judgment upon them, he absorbed it into the depths of his divine humanity.

Campbell now turns to the prospective side. Through his whole atoning life the Son was bearing witness to the Father's purpose and desire that all men should walk before him as dear children. " What it is to be a man, what we possess in humanity, we never know until we see humanity in Him who through the eternal Spirit offered himself without spot to God . . . in the beloved Son is the Father seen to be well pleased, and in our being through him to the Father dear children will it come to pass that the Father will be well pleased in us." And this whole process comes to a focus in Jesus' prayer life in which he constantly offers himself afresh to the Father in filial obedience. Finally the Son's dealing with the Father on our behalf must be regarded, in its prospective aspect, as a supreme act of intercession. He himself has delighted to do the Father's will from within humanity. He knows that it is the Father's will that all men should walk before him as dear children; with what confidence, then, can he offer intercession on our behalf that what he has himself experienced while living as man may be reproduced in those who, by their very nature, must live as men! In his completed experience of obedient sonship within humanity, he provides the ground for an intercession which can continually arise to the Father: " Father, I will that they whom thou hast given me may so walk even as I have walked." That intercession was expressed, not simply in words, but in his whole human experience culminating in the cross.

Thus it becomes possible for us to speak of the cross as the

Great Confessional and as the Great Intercessional. It confesses God's judgment on human sin; it confesses, from within humanity, that that judgment is holy and righteous. It reveals God's eternal purpose that men should walk before him as obedient children; it intercedes from within humanity, that that purpose may be fulfilled. There may be many difficulties in following Campbell's entire exposition of the nature of the atonement, but his use of the common experiences of confession and intercession to throw light upon the saving work of Christ is surely one of the most fruitful insights in the whole history of inquiry into its inner meaning. In his prayers Jesus' inner character and purpose achieved their fullest expression. He honored his Father to the uttermost; he loved his brethren to the uttermost. To his brethren he revealed the heart of the Father; to his Father he revealed the heart of a true human son. In and through his prayers the holy Father and the erring sons were brought together and made one. He is our peace and through him we walk before God as dear children, we have access to the Father through the Spirit, and we rejoice in hope of the final experience of the glorious liberty of the sons of God.

" Almighty God, whose most dear Son went not up to joy but first he suffered pain, and entered not into glory before he was crucified; Mercifully grant that we, walking in the way of the cross, may find it none other than the way of life and peace; through the same thy Son Jesus Christ our Lord. Amen."

— From The Book of Common Prayer.

CHAPTER V

THE SIN BEARER

" O blessed Jesu, how hast Thou offended,
  That now on Thee such judgment has descended?
  Of what misdeed hast Thou to make confession?
      Of what transgression?

.   .   .   .

" My sin it is which binds Thee,
  With anguish deep surrounds Thee,
  And nails Thee to the Tree;
  The torture Thou art feeling,
  Thy patient love revealing,
  'Tis I should bear it, I alone."

It is not easy for us to realize today how great was the task of the early Christian preachers as they sought to interpret to new converts or to those interested in becoming converts the meaning of the inescapable fact that the Christ had suffered under Pontius Pilate, been crucified, dead, and buried. Today the cross has become a symbol of glory more than of disgrace, but in the first century there was little of glory attached to it. The brutal punishment meted out to a criminal offender — this was the natural reaction to any talk of a cross in the days of imperial Rome.

There can be little doubt that the chief assistance to those wrestling with the problem of undeserved suffering and shame came to them from examining more carefully than hitherto the implications of these Old Testament passages that were concerned with the same problem. Nowhere did the parallels seem closer than in the records of the career of God's righteous Servant, contained in the latter part of The Book of Isaiah. His had been an experience of affliction and distress and yet out of it all there had come final vindication and the fulfillment of God's own purpose. In the gallery of Old Testament portraits none can have received more attention in the early days of the Christian Church than the noble figure of the Suffering Servant of Isa., ch. 53.

But as they gazed at this portrait one feature seemed to make a deeper impression upon them than any other. It was the sight of this man bearing upon his own back the great weary weight of the world's burden of sin and shame. One New Testament interpreter indeed sees in the picture a prevision of the healing ministry of Jesus, in which he seemed to take upon himself the sicknesses and infirmities of men and thereby to bring them relief. But in the main the weight that had to be borne was that of human rebellion and the punishment which it entailed. *Ours* was the pain he bore, because we had sinned; *we* had all gone astray, and the Lord "laid on him the iniquity of us all"; the Lord's servant shall "justify many," for *theirs* are the sins that he bore. He "let himself be numbered among rebels, bearing the great world's sins, and interposing for rebellious men" (Moffatt). These are the cries of the prophet as he envisages the innocent sufferer bearing the great world's sins and these are the phrases that find their echoes in the snatches of the preaching of the early Christian witnesses which the early narratives contain.

Take for example the incident recorded in Acts, ch. 8. Here the way is already prepared, for the devout seeker has been meditating upon the prophetic writings to which we have already referred. "He was led as a sheep to the slaughter; and like a lamb dumb before his shearer, so opened he not his mouth. . . . Of whom speaketh the prophet this? . . . Then Philip . . . preached unto him Jesus." Or take a more extended section from what is probably an early Christian sermon in I Peter, ch. 2:

"Christ also suffered for us, leaving us an example, that ye should follow his steps: Who did no sin, neither was guile found in his mouth: Who when he was reviled, reviled not again; when he suffered, he threatened not; but committed himself to him that judgeth righteously: Who his own self bare our sins in his own body on the tree, that we, being dead to sins, should live unto righteousness: by whose stripes ye were healed."

Here the echoes of Isa., ch. 53, are unmistakable and the burden motif is the most prominent feature of all. One further example may be found at the conclusion of the ninth chapter of The Epistle to the Hebrews. In a short summary the author draws his argument together and emphasizes the once-for-all character of Christ's work with deep solemnity:

" Now once in the end of the world hath he appeared to put away sin by the sacrifice of himself. And as it is appointed unto men once to die, but after this the judgment: So Christ was once offered to bear the sins of many; and unto them that look for him shall he appear the second time without sin unto salvation."

" *To bear the sins of many.*" This phrase which echoes Isa., ch. 53, seems to have burned itself into the consciousness of these early preachers. The Messiah, the Son of God, had come in the form of a servant and had fulfilled the servant's task of bearing the burdens of many. He had carried their burdens of anxiety and infirmity, he had carried the cross laid upon his shoulders by their indifference and obtuseness, he had carried the great burden of the world's sin. In a striking Christian sermon preached in the year A.D. 1606, Lancelot Andrewes takes the verse from Isa., ch. 53, and translates it: " He hath laid upon his shoulders the iniquity of us all." Ordinary things, he comments, we carry in our arms or lift at the arms' end; it must be very heavy if we must put shoulders and all to it. " Come, saith He, you that are heavy laden, and I will refresh you by loading myself; take it from your necks and lay it on mine own. His suffering, though it grew so heavy as it wrung from him plenty of tears, and a strong cry, a sweat of blood — such was the weight of it — yet would he not cast it off, but there held it still, till it made him bow down his head and give up the ghost."

Thus, through the centuries, men have turned to the picture of the world's sin bearer, first painted by the ancient Hebrew prophet, and have found in it solace and release. How far this picture sustained the souls of faithful Israelites in earlier days we have no means of knowing. But as soon as the One appeared who on the plane of history stepped out from the picture, as it were, into the world of human need, the song of release began to ascend and men knew that the bearing of sins was no longer in the realm of vision but of reality. He bare our sins up into his own body on the tree — no sentence more simply and yet more movingly declares the faith of the early Christians that the burden of guilt was no longer theirs to carry just because the Christ had laid it on his own shoulders and borne it away.

THE SCAPEGOAT

It is time, however, to inquire a little more closely into the origins of this belief that the Christ was able to take upon his own shoulders the sins of mankind. In simple terms we may say that the belief has taken shape in the pattern of a particular *image* and that the particular image took shape out of a common *experience* shared by men the world over. The common experience is that of transferring a weight from human backs to some other carrier, animate or inanimate. For example, a man found that he could load a weight onto a raft and make it his carrier; or he could tame an animal and make it bear his burden; or he could even compel another human being to take from him that which he had no desire to carry himself. It was a short step from this common experience to *imagine* that weights of other kinds could be transferred in similar fashion and that, if only the proper substitute could be found, man's psychical existence as well as his physical could be made buoyant and light. At the beginning of the volume dealing with the scapegoat in his great work *The Golden Bough,* Sir James Frazer puts the matter very tersely. " Because it is possible to shift a load of wood, stones, or what not, from our own back to the back of another, the savage fancies that it is equally possible to shift the burden of his pains and sorrows to another, who will suffer them in his stead. Upon this idea he acts, and the result is an endless number of very unamiable devices for palming off upon someone else the trouble which a man shrinks from bearing himself. In short, the principle of vicarious suffering is commonly understood and practiced by races who stand on a low level of social and intellectual culture."

It is well to emphasize at this point that an image need not be despised because of its lowly origins or because of its possible abuses. There is nothing wrong in a man's utilizing the forces of nature to assist him in bearing his burdens. Normally there need be nothing amiss in employing an animal such as a horse or a camel for the same purpose. The animal, of course, must be properly treated, and this is even true of the mechanical devices that man may construct to assist him in his purposes. But it could be argued that man's greatest advances have been made possible by his discovery of adequate substitutes to bear his burdens for him and to carry the loads that would otherwise have exhausted and defeated him. The matter becomes much more delicate when we think in terms of human burden bearers, but even here there is nothing intrinsically wrong in one man's being employed to bear, or at least to share, the burden of another. To be a burden bearer can be one of the noblest of all human callings — though it can also be one of the most degrading. All we are affirming is that the original experience lying behind the formation of the image is one of the most significant and one of the most creative within man's historical development.

Coming nearer to its use in the "Servant songs" of Isaiah and in the New Testament writings, we find that the idea of a transference of a more-than-physical burden to another gained wide acceptance both in the Hellenistic and in the Jewish worlds in the last centuries B.C. Sir James Frazer, in the volume to which we have already referred, casts his net far and wide in the endeavor to collect examples of the scapegoat motif in primitive cultures in different parts of the world. But he pays special attention to the civilization of Greece and Rome, and what he has to say about Greece is of particular interest to us as we consider the background of the Biblical image. Giving examples from various centers of Greek civilization, he writes: "Whenever Marseilles, one of the busiest and most brilliant of Greek colonies, was ravaged by a plague, a man of the poorer classes used to offer himself as a scapegoat. For a whole year he was maintained at the public expense, being fed on choice and pure food. At the expiry of the year he was dressed in sacred garments, decked with holy branches, and led through the whole city, while prayers were uttered that all the evils of the people might fall on his head. He was then cast out of the city or stoned to death by the people outside of the walls. The Athenians regularly maintained a number of degraded and useless beings at the public expense; and when any calamity, such as plague, drought, or famine, befell the city, they sacrificed two of these outcasts as scapegoats. One of the victims was sacrificed for the men and the other for the women. The former wore round his neck a string of black, the latter a string of white figs. Sometimes, it seems, the victim slain on behalf of the women was a woman. They were led about the city and then sacrificed, apparently by being stoned to death outside the city. But such sacrifices were not confined to extraordinary occasions of public calamity; it appears that every year, at the festival of the Thargelia in May, two victims, one for the men and one for the women, were led out of Athens and stoned to death. The city of Abdera in Thrace was publicly purified once a year, and one of the burghers, set apart for the purpose, was stoned to death as a scapegoat or vicarious sacrifice for the life of all the others; six days before his execution he was excommunicated 'in order that he alone might bear the sins of all the people'" (pp. 253–254).

This was the climate into which Christianity came. There was the sense that diseases, misfortunes, misdemeanors, ritual faults, were ever accumulating and that periodically it was essential for any society to rid itself of these ills by some form of open and public expulsion. The simple expedient of transferring the load from the society at large to the shoulders of a single victim was commonly employed and thereby, it was believed, a thorough purification was effected. In some cases the victim was compelled to fulfill the scapegoat role, but often, it appears, the function was regarded as an honorable one and there was no difficulty in finding a candidate who was willing to offer himself for the task.

But though there were these patterns of imagination already in existence in the Hellenistic world, it is to the practices of later Judaism that we must look for our main source of the scapegoat idea. Here the material is clearly set forth in the book of Leviticus and two passages are specially worthy of attention. The first is that which contains the directions for the cleansing of a leper. If the plague has disappeared, " then shall the priest command to take for him that is to be cleansed two birds alive and clean, and cedar wood, and scarlet, and hyssop: and the priest shall command that one of the birds be killed in an earthen vessel over running water. As for the living bird, he shall take it, and the cedar wood, and the scarlet, and the hyssop, and shall dip them and the living bird in the blood of the bird that was killed over the running water: and he shall sprinkle upon him that is to be cleansed from the leprosy seven times, and shall pronounce him clean, and shall let the living bird loose into the open field " (Lev. 14:4–7). Whatever uncertainties there may be about the meaning of some of the details of the ritual, it seems clear that the living bird let loose into the open fields was regarded as carrying away the leprosy with him. It was, it would seem, in the nature of an extra precautionary measure to make sure that no traces of the disease were left behind.

Of far greater importance, however, is the record of the Day of Atonement ceremonies in Lev., ch. 16. In addition to a bullock and a ram two kids of the goats had to be taken by the high priest as sin offering: " And he shall take the two goats, and present them before the Lord at the door of the tabernacle of the congregation. And Aaron shall cast lots upon the two goats; one lot for the Lord, and the other lot for the scapegoat. And Aaron shall bring the goat upon which the Lord's lot fell, and offer him for a sin offering. But the goat, on which the lot fell to be the scapegoat, shall be presented alive before the Lord, to make an atonement with him, and to let him go for a scapegoat into the wilderness " (Lev. 16:7–10). At a later point in the chapter more is told us about the scapegoat: " And Aaron shall lay both his hands upon the head of the live goat, and confess over him all the iniquities of the children of Israel, and all their transgressions in all their sins, putting them upon the head of the goat, and shall send him away by the hand of a fit man into the wilderness: and the goat shall bear upon him all their iniquities unto a land not inhabited: and he shall let go the goat in the wilderness " (vs. 21, 22).

The significance of this dramatic ritual is not difficult to discern. It bears a number of parallels to the ceremonial practices of other tribes, and we are justified in believing that it shared with them the purpose of cleansing the whole community from the accumulated guilt and defilement of a particular period of time. It is interesting that in Israel the victim was an animal and not a human being, and that it was not actually killed but sent out to almost certain destruction amidst the perils of the wilderness. It is also interesting to note that the transference of guilt was no merely mechanical performance but was effected by means of a solemn confession of sin over the head of the animal. In later Judaism the Day of Atonement was one of the most solemn days of the year, and in the dramatic ceremonial of the day no section could have been more impressive than that which was concerned with the goat. In the popular imagination it was the goat that bore the sins and carried the sorrows far away into a land of desolation and destruction. At this point the individual was relieved of the necessity of bearing his own iniquity: the scapegoat was laden with it all.

A Picture and Its Meaning

One of the profoundest interpreters of the cross in the early years of this century was the great theologian Peter Taylor Forsyth. Though respected in his own day, it is only recently that his essential message of life through death, of light through darkness, seems to have made its full impact upon the minds of men. He steadfastly refused to be swept along by any shallow tide of contemporary optimism but kept his eyes upon the cross and the resurrection, the only hope of final victory in the long travail of the ages. Forsyth was an exceedingly versatile man, being not only an outstanding theologian and philosopher but also a critic and interpreter of art. One of his lesser known books is *Religion in Recent Art,* and in this he acknowledges his special indebtedness to one of the great artists of the nineteenth century, Holman Hunt. In Forsyth's judgment, Hunt had done for Protestant painting what Bach did for Protestant music. Not so much the passion and tragedy of death but the victory of life over death is the subject of his painting. He paints the cross, says Forsyth, in the spirit of the resurrection. He sees the color even in shadow. The very darkness of death he makes beautiful by his firm faith in the ulterior issues of death. At the very center of his art is the Christ that died, nay, rather, that is risen again and ever lives to make intercession for us.

Probably Holman Hunt's best known painting is *The Light of the World*. But Forsyth chooses three others which he believes are all concerned with the one doctrine of the atonement. These three are *The Scapegoat, The Shadow of Death,* and *The Triumph of the Innocents*. The first two "deal with the cross in the light of this toiling mortal world, the third in the light of another world, radiant and immortal." We shall confine our attention to the very remarkable picture *The Scapegoat*.

Let us first attempt a brief description of it. In the background there is a chain of mountains glowing in rich colors as it is touched by the rays of the setting sun. These are the mountains of Abarim, from which Moses viewed the Promised Land. The sky is bright above them, and the whole view suggests the glory of the divine creation. But this is only the background. From the foot of the mountains, stretching forward to the front edge of the picture, there is a very different scene. The waters of the Dead Sea are dark, for they reflect a storm cloud overhead. Everything suggests barrenness and a curse. On the surface of the waters there is gloom; beneath them, we know, lie the ruins of a dead civilization. At the water's edge there is nothing but sterility: a dead branch caked with salt, the skull of a dead animal protruding from the shallows, the shore a lifeless waste. And then at the very center of the desolation there stands the unutterably pathetic creature the scapegoat. The shaggy, heavy creature is at its last gasp. "We mark," says Forsyth, "the trembling forelegs at their last step, the depressed head, the low back, and the outspread hind legs (as if the weakness were no mere sinking of failure, but the pressure of a world of inevitable load), the bleeding footprints broken into the caked soil — the record of a long, long journey from Zion and its peace, through a land where ' no man comes nor hath come, since the making of the world.' We see the bent and smitten head, the dull, dying eye, the parched and gasping mouth." In this dumb and patient creature there seems to be gathered up " the curse unspeakable, the intolerable weight, and the agonized sin-bearing of all the dull, weary, and evil world." Finally, and its significance must not be forgotten, there is the rainbow of unearthly glory encircling the whole scene and redeeming it from hopelessness and final despair.

It would be foolish to imagine that a single picture could fully express the mystery of the atoning work of Christ and it would be useless to dwell overmuch on points of detail. Yet few symbols could express more powerfully the overwhelming weight of the burden that the Redeemer of mankind bore upon his heart. As Forsyth points out, it is not the purpose of a symbol or picture to express through an exact correspondence of detail the reality which it is intended to convey. Often it needs to be no more than a hint or a suggestion. The all-important thing is that it should stir the imagination and permit the light of some new truth to dawn upon the soul. So with this picture, its main purpose has been achieved if it opens our eyes ever so little to see afresh the awful reality of sin's curse upon nature and upon man which the Saviour so willingly bore.

The picture would be profoundly moving were *any* representative of the animal creation depicted in the goat's predicament. But the artist has a particular animal in mind — the scapegoat, with all the associations of the Day of Atonement. What does this imply? We cannot know the artist's mind, but at least to Forsyth it suggested the profoundest interpretation of the work of Christ that he could imagine. These are his words: " The goat went out loaded, not with individual guilt, but with the curse of a nation's sin, just as Christ went out bearing, not the *guilt* (for he was pure — the creature was harmless), but the mysterious curse and load of sin as it presses upon the whole world. In the oldest times the goat was supposed to carry the sin and curse back to the great deity that was its author. The Christian thought is that Christ carried the horror and curse of the sin, amid fearful loneliness and agony, into the presence of God by confession full and complete; where the sin, being thus exposed, was purged and burned away in the forgiving love of God who is a consuming fire. Mind after mind, in the solemnized exercise of spiritual imagination, has tried to pierce with sympathy the darkness of Gethsemane, to gauge with amazement the nature of the Saviour's woe, and humbly to bear if it were but the corner of his garment under the load of this curse unspeakable. It is a task too great for human power. Fully to gauge those sorrows would be fully to bear them. Fully to express them would be fully to confess them; the thing no man could do, else the God-Man had not come to do it on our behalf. . . . What we have here, then, is a most wonderful and successful symbol, not artificial but natural, not conventional but original, not fanciful but a part of the reality — a symbol with sacramental power to convey the staggering horror of spiritual curse, and the awful strain of the sin-bearing which takes sin away."

The picture is grimly realistic but it is not a picture of despair. In fact, it is ultimately a picture of promise and hope. There is no hiding of the blight and the barrenness of the world's sin. The desert has supplanted the sown, the salty ooze has replaced the fresh and living water, the creature of death stands as the only symbol of life under the curse. Yet all is not desolation. At least there is the sin bearer; at least there is the bow with its promise of blessing; at least there is " the light of the glory of God in the face of Jesus Christ." The awfulness of bearing the burden of the world's sin cannot be minimized. Yet it only serves to enhance the wonder of the act of the Burden Bearer, who willingly took up and shouldered and bore away into everlasting oblivion the sin of the world.

The Lamb of God

Although, as we have seen, it is possible to draw a comparison between Christ the Sin Bearer and the goat laden with the sins of the people, this is never actually done in the New Testament. Instead of a goat, a lamb is chosen. Already there rings out the cry that was to become one of the most familiar themes of later Christian worship: " Behold the Lamb of God! " Of all the symbols that have established themselves in the consciousness of Christendom possibly none has been more precious than that of the Lamb of God who bears away the sins of the world. One of the oldest Christian hymns, the Gloria in Excelsis, has as its central cry:

" O Lord God, Lamb of God, Son of the Father, That takest away the sins of the world: have mercy upon us. Thou that takest away the sins of the world: receive our prayer."

This hymn was being sung in the East as early as the third century A.D., and Dom Gregory Dix has told us that the idea of the Lamb of God attracted a special devotion in the Syrian Church. At the end of the seventh century the then pope, who was a Syrian by birth, introduced into the Roman Eucharistic rite the little hymn:

" O Lamb of God, that takest away the sins of the world, have mercy upon us,"

and this has remained a part of the Roman Mass ever since.

But not only has the adoration of the Lamb constituted a prominent part of liturgical worship; it has also figured in the great hymns of the Protestant Churches. What could be simpler yet finer than Isaac Watts's verse:

" ' Worthy the Lamb that died,' they cry,
' To be exalted thus! '
' Worthy the Lamb! ' our hearts reply,
' For He was slain for us.' "

What could be more daring in its imagery, yet confident in its
hope than Charles Wesley's:

> " What though a thousand hosts engage,
>   A thousand worlds, my soul to shake?
> I have a shield shall quell their rage,
>   And drive the alien armies back;
> Portrayed it bears a bleeding Lamb:
> I dare believe in Jesus' name " ?

The slain Lamb, the victorious Lamb, the burdened Lamb, the
enthroned Lamb — these have been the themes of Christian
hymnody throughout the centuries.

But the Lamb has also been one of the favorite subjects for
Christian art. Two of the earliest known Christian symbolic forms
portray the Lamb. In one the Lamb is in a recumbent position,
lying on the book of seven seals; in the other he stands erect and
carries the banner of victory. The symbol was common in the
Roman catacombs, and in his book on Christian symbolism,
Dr. Thomas A. Stafford suggests that this is the greatest of all symbols used in Christian art to represent the Son of God. After the
Edict of Toleration in the early part of the fourth century A.D., the
Lamb came to be a constant object of contemplation and representation, perhaps because no other symbol so adequately represented the
double-sidedness of the work of Christ. He had been slain in sacrifice and yet he was conquering and triumphant. He who had
borne the sins of the world was also the leader who would bring
his people to final victory. It is fitting that we should examine in
more detail the origins of this symbol which has established itself so securely in the imagination and devotion of Christendom.

Although the Lamb has often been associated with the sacrificial
system of the Old Testament, it seems altogether more probable
that the background of the New Testament references is to be
found rather in the great chapter to which we have already referred — Isa., ch. 53. In this we read that the Servant was led like
a sheep to the slaughter and as a ewe before her shearers is dumb.
(In the Greek version of the Old Testament the word used for

ewe is *amnos,* which would normally be translated " lamb.") Thus
if, as we have reason to believe, Jesus was from the earliest days
of Christian preaching identified with the Servant of the songs
of Isaiah, it was only natural that a metaphor used of the Servant
should have been transferred to Jesus himself. For had he not in
very truth been led as a sheep to the slaughter and had he not remained silent in his affliction like the lamb in the hands of its
shearers? And seeing that in the Servant song the burden of the
guilty was said to have been laid upon the shoulders of the
innocent, it was only natural to speak of the lamb as the sin bearer:
The Sheep or Lamb of God had borne away the sin of the world.

But although we may find suggestions of the sheep or lamb
metaphor in the use of the fifty-third chapter of Isaiah in the
Early Church, it needed a particular writer to take the image and
establish it firmly as one of Christianity's leading symbolic forms.
Such a writer was the literary artist who composed The Revelation
of John the Divine. The author of this book, whom we shall call
the seer, took the lamb symbol and used it some twenty-eight
times in reference to Christ. In the context of his writing the
symbol is specially apt and appealing, for the powers that are
threatening to destroy the infant Church can best be compared to
the wild beasts who obey the laws of the jungle. Over against
them stands a Lamb — and yet the Lamb is the conqueror. Or,
again, in the great passage where the lamb symbol is first introduced there is a dramatic contrast between the Lion and the
Lamb. He who sits on the throne holds in his right hand a book
of mystery sealed with seven seals. To the seer's distress, no one
is found capable of opening the book. At length one of the elders
in the heavenly court assures him that the Lion of the tribe of
Judah (a notable Jewish Messianic title) has prevailed to open the
book. Yet immediately we are told that " a Lamb as it had been
slain " came and took the book. Not a lion but a Lamb, not the
king of the beasts but the most defenseless and helpless of domestic animals, not a lion in the fullness of his natural strength
but a Lamb in the virture of his willing sacrifice — this is the
One who possesses all wisdom and is in full control. He *is* the

Messiah, he *is* Judah's champion, and yet he is not the kind of messianic champion whom the Jews expected. The Lamb brought to the slaughter is the One who has been highly exalted and who is now King and Lord forevermore.

Having introduced the Lamb in this dramatic fashion, the seer proceeds to break out in songs of praise to the Lamb. Whether those hymns were composed by the seer himself or were already current in early Christian hymnody, they form some of the noblest anthems of our Christian heritage.

> "Worthy art thou . . . :
> For thou wast slain,
> And hast redeemed unto God with thy blood
> Men of every tribe, and tongue, and people, and nation (Rev. 5:9).

> "Worthy is the Lamb that was slain
> To receive the power, and riches, and wisdom,
> And might, and honor, and glory, and blessing (v. 12).

> "Unto him that sitteth on the throne, and unto the Lamb,
> Be the blessing, and the honor, and the glory,
> And the power, for ever and ever " (v. 13).

In the subsequent chapters of Revelation, the seer moves backward and forward between his two main themes. The Lamb was slain, the Lamb shed his blood, the Lamb has redeemed men of all nations; the Lamb is in the midst of the throne, the Lamb is judge of all, the Lamb leads men in triumph to their true destiny. The Lamb slain — this was the symbol that was capable of inspiring unlimited outpourings of grateful devotion; the Lamb enthroned — this was the symbol that was capable of arousing the deepest feelings of reverent awe and glad obedience. Not so much is said of the Lamb in his relation to sin, though the wider testimony of the book is plain that the Christ through his sacrificial death and costly blood-shedding had loosed men from their sins and made them kings and priests to God his Father. But we cannot affirm that Revelation depicts the Lamb as the Sin Bearer; first and foremost he is the Redeemer, the Victor wounded in the fight, the Leader, the King.

It is in another book written in the closing years of the first century that we find the explicit reference to the Lamb of God who takes away the sin of the world. In the first chapter of John's Gospel, the Baptist bears his witness to Jesus of Nazareth in these terms. Again the memory of Isa., ch. 53, has probably determined the form of the expression, though there may be a secondary reference to the Passover lamb which was offered in sacrifice (though not as a sin offering). In all probability this particular cry, " Behold the Lamb of God, that taketh away the sin of the world," was by the time of the Gospel's composition being used in the worship services of the Church, and just as the potential disciples of Jesus by the River Jordan were bidden to behold the Lamb, so later in regularly established worship the congregation may have been exhorted in the same terms: " Prepare yourselves to worship God! Prepare yourselves to receive the Holy Spirit! Behold the Lamb of God that beareth away the sin of the world! "

Thus in the New Testament and in Christian antiquity men did not point to Jesus as the scapegoat who had borne his people's guilt away into a land of desolation. Rather, they pointed to him as the Lamb of God who, following the example of the lamblike servant of the Isaianic songs, bore the sins and carried the iniquities of many. They did not ask *how* it had been possible for one to carry the burdens of others. They knew that their own guilt had been a weight too heavy to be borne; they knew that they could not remove it themselves; they knew of no earthly power, no system, no rite, no mediator, able to bring them relief. But what if God himself had sent his Servant to assume the load and carry it away to a place of annulment? What if there was a Lamb of God who, in ways impossible to explain, had taken mankind's unjustified rebellion upon himself and had thereby absorbed it? So the cry has gone on re-echoing through the ages:

> " Behold the Lamb of God, that
> taketh away the sin of the world!
> O Lamb of God, that takest away
> the sins of the world, have
> mercy upon us.

O Lamb of God, that takest away
the sins of the world, grant
us Thy peace."

In Sholem Asch's novel *Mary,* Jesus' mother is on her way up
to Jerusalem in company with the beloved disciple. "When they
reached the heights of Mount Scopus, whence Jerusalem could be
seen in the distance, her guide stopped. It was early morning and
the sun was up over the Holy City. Far away its white façades
basked in the young light, and the gold and bronzen turrets of
the Temple gates gleamed on the hill of Moriah. They were both
gazing at the city, and then it was Jochanan who spoke:

"'Woman,' he said, 'see you what I see over Jerusalem?'

"'What do you see, Jochanan?' asked Miriam.

"'I see what Moses saw in the desert. But it is not a burning
bush; it is a lamb. All the mountains of the earth strain toward
Mount Moriah. But Moriah soars above them all, and on it stands
the House of God, and high upon its dome I see a fiery altar, the
stone of Moriah. And on the altar stands God's sacrifice and it
burns and burns with fire and is not consumed.'

"Miriam paled.

"'What is this sacrifice, Jochanan?'

"'It is the lamb of God that burns unconsumed in perpetual
fire.'"

The imagery may not entirely correspond with that of the
Bible, but the underlying insight is altogether true. To bear away
the sins of the world is no light and easy task. Sacrifice, the fire,
the cross — these are all symbols of the travail of the Lamb of
God. But out of the travail of his soul he sees the light of victory
and he is satisfied.

"Worthy is the Lamb that hath been slain to receive the powers and
riches, and wisdom, and might, and honour, and glory and blessing.
Unto the Lamb be glory!

"Unto Him that sitteth on the throne, and unto the Lamb, be the blessing, and the honour, and the glory and the dominon for ever and ever.

Unto the Lamb be glory!

" Worthy art thou, for thou wast slain, and didst purchase unto God with thy blood men of every tribe, and tongue, and people, and nation.

Unto the Lamb be glory! "

— *From the Service of the Lord's Supper*
Authorized by the Church of South India.

Chapter VI

THE GREAT HIGH PRIEST

" Where high the heavenly temple stands,
    The house of God not made with hands,
    A great High-Priest our nature wears,
    The Saviour of mankind appears.

" He who for men their surety stood,
    And pour'd on earth His precious Blood,
    Pursues in heav'n His mighty plan,
    The Saviour and the Friend of man."

In an earlier chapter we suggested that a great change has taken place in the interpretation of the meaning of the death of Christ during the past century. Whereas previously the context of interpretation had been the courts of justice or the field of battle, about a century ago men began to look to the worship of the sanctuary or to the practice of private prayer, seeking to discover in those areas patterns of the great action of atonement achieved by God in Christ. We have already considered the interpretation that can be made in terms of deep, personal, agonizing prayer. Let us now turn our thoughts to public worship, and in particular to sacrificial worship, which has played so central a part in the whole religious history of mankind.

The work of Christ may be regarded as the offering of the full, perfect, and sufficient sacrifice: this statement, it may be confidently affirmed, would command almost universal assent. But as soon as the attempt is made to expand the term " sacrifice " — to discuss the nature of sacrifice, to examine the essential meaning of sacrifice, to consider the actions and methods appropriate to sacrifice — we find ourselves in the midst of the widest possible divergences of opinion. Some, for example, find it impossible to think of sacrifice without conjuring up visions of an offended deity and of an offering being made to appease him or to satisfy his just demands. Others think simply in terms of a special act of grateful response to a deity who has shown favor to his worshipers. Still others recognize that sacrifice is in some way connected with the continuing life of the universe: in sacrifice there is a constant dramatic representation of the principle that new life can come only through death, that "except a corn of wheat fall into the ground and die, it abideth alone: but if it die, it bringeth forth much fruit." Here are radically different conceptions of sacrifice, and much of the difficulty of establishing agreement, even in Christian circles, on the question of the way of salvation derives from confusion and uncertainty about the meaning of sacrifice. It is important therefore that we should first try to clarify some of the points at issue.

In the first place it needs to be said with all possible emphasis that to interpret sacrifice solely or even primarily in terms of propitiation, appeasement, or penal offering is to go contrary both to the Biblical revelation and to the deepest religious instincts of mankind. This is not to deny that there is value in holding fast to the conviction that God cannot be mocked, that transgressions of his law cannot be treated lightly, and that some act of reparation by those who have offended may be a morally healthy thing. But to erect this conviction into a formal system and to prescribe sacrifices of propitiation and restitution for every known offense is to make religion wholly mechanical and to create a God who is simply a remote enforcer of public laws. This, in effect, was the situation in ancient Rome, and it is from this source that the idea of sacrifice as penal and propitiatory has largely been drawn. It is true that there are references to sin offerings and guilt offerings in the book of Leviticus and it has easily been imagined that these fit into the same general category as the sacrifices prescribed by Roman law. In point of fact, however, these particular sacrifices constituted only one part of the Old Testament sacrificial system and in any case the idea that lay behind them was not exactly the same as that which directed the observances of the Roman people.

In the second place it needs also to be said that it is not sufficient to interpret sacrifice in a purely *spiritual* way. Wherever sacrifice has formed a regular part of religious worship (and this has been the case in almost every known form of religion), it has been concerned with open actions and concrete objects. The objects offered in sacrifice have varied from things of apparently trifling value up to a man's own body or the body of one he loves. But in every case there has been some externalization; otherwise the term " sacrifice " could not have been used in any meaningful way. Certainly there can be a silent offering of love or adoration, but it is confusing to call that a sacrifice. In fact, to speak of sacrifice when no outward action is involved and no concrete offering is made is a misuse of the term. Even when the New Testament speaks of " spiritual sacrifices," or of a " sacrifice of praise," it is altogether likely that some external action is in view. There are times and places when it becomes almost impossible to make an offering in an outward and visible way but in those cases it is best either to avoid the use of the term " sacrifice " or to make it clear that it is being used in an unusual and strictly limited fashion.

Between the two extremes of formalized external activity and formless internal devotion there lies a wide field of sacrificial worship whose general character can be briefly described. It rests upon the fundamental belief that man cannot be independent either of the natural order within which he lives or of the society to which he belongs or of the divine being or beings on whose providence he depends. He may try to cut himself off from either of these contexts but, in so far as he succeeds, he finds that his life is impoverished, distorted, and ultimately damaged beyond repair. Complete independence is impossible. But if this is so, how is a true dependence to be maintained? The answer essentially is that only through a process of give-and-take within these interlocking contexts can wholeness of life be maintained. Sacrifice is an intense, dramatic realization and representation of the process that must either be going on all the time or constantly be repeated in order that life's interrelationships may continue sound and strong. Things from the realm of nature are both taken by the society and offered to the deity and received by the society as gifts from the deity.

Normally in the history of religion the ordering of sacrificial worship has been the task of a regular priesthood. In its simplest forms sacrifice may have been offered by the head of the household or the chief of the tribe, but even in these cases one man has acted in a certain representative capacity. At a very early stage in the development of the rite certain men seem to have been appointed to perform the proper ceremonial and to recite the appropriate formulas, and they naturally came to be regarded as occupying a mediating position between the worshipers on the one side and the deity on the other. They performed certain acts toward the deity on behalf of the people; they performed certain acts toward the people on behalf of the deity. It is important that we should know what the general nature of these acts was, especially in the priestly system that is described in the Old Testament.

Recent studies have made it clear that in the offering of sacrifice any worshiper could bring his particular gift to the sanctuary. If the gift were an animal, he himself slew it and then presented it to the priest; if the gift were fruit or grain, it was presented directly. The first task of the priest was to act carefully and correctly in handling the blood of the slain animal. The blood was the seat of life and was most precious; on no account could it be treated in any casual way. Sometimes the blood was directed toward the deity alone, sometimes toward both the deity and his worshipers. The second task was to deal with the offerings themselves. Here the precise action depended both upon the type of sacrifice that was being performed and upon the nature of the gifts. But in all cases there was some form of dedication to the deity: the offering might be burned upon the altar or it might be waved in the air or it might be lifted up while certain words were recited. In conclusion, specified parts of the offering were distributed by the priests to the people and the normal ending of the whole ceremony was a solemn feast in which both the priests and the people took part.

It is in the light of what we have said about sacrifice and priesthood that we shall now consider the New Testament references to our Lord's sacrifice and his eternal priesthood. Outside The

Epistle to the Hebrews the references are scanty. We know that Ps. 110 played a considerable part in the apologetic of the Early Church and it portrays the Messiah as priest as well as king. It has been customary to call the prayer of John, ch. 17, the great high-priestly prayer of Christ, but the designation priest is nowhere used in the text. Thus, apart from inferences that we may legitimately draw from sacrificial ideas found in other parts of the New Testament, we shall depend mainly upon The Epistle to the Hebrews for our interpretations of this aspect of our Lord's ministry.

The Blood of Christ

The references to the blood of Christ in the New Testament are so striking as to demand careful attention. First and foremost we have the accounts of the Last Supper, in which Jesus took a cup of wine and said, " This is my blood of the new testament, which is shed for many." Then in the Pauline writings we have the exceedingly important verse, Rom. 3:25, in which the apostle refers to God's having set forth Christ Jesus openly as a means of expiation through his blood; in Ephesians and Colossians there are parallel references to redemption and peace through the blood of the cross. In I Peter there is a further reference to redemption by " the precious blood of Christ," and we find that this is also the key thought in two of the anthems of the book of Revelation. In the Johannine writings the most famous reference is that of I John 1:7: " The blood of Jesus Christ his Son cleanseth us from all sin "; and in The Acts, that of ch. 20:28: " The church of God, which he hath purchased with his own blood."

What main lines of interpretation can we offer of these various sayings? Viewing them all together, we see that the main notes of emphasis are those of redemption, cleansing, and the covenant. As regards the first, everything points back to the Exodus record of the redemption of the Children of Israel from the bondage of Egypt. In this record, the ritual actions with the lamb are at the center of the picture. A lamb without blemish is taken, its blood is sprinkled on the side posts and upper doorpost of the house by the head of the family, and thereby the household is incorporated into the whole company of the people who are to be redeemed by God. On the morrow they go forth out of the land of Egypt into the freedom of a new life. This picture was regarded by the early Christians as a dramatic foreshadowing of their own experience. Had they not been held fast by the bondage of the world, the flesh, and the devil? Had not the Lamb of God, without spot and without blemish, offered his blood to separate them from the power and influence of all evil forces and to bring them into the company of God's redeemed people? Had they not gone forth into the freedom of the children of God, redeemed by the precious blood of Christ?

As regards the ideas of cleansing and covenant, it will be best to consider them in the context of The Epistle to the Hebrews, to which we now turn. In the ninth chapter of this Epistle, two Old Testament scenes provide the material for the author's comparisons and expositions. The first is the Day of Atonement ceremony in which the high priest plays the chief part. The ritual with blood is quite complex. The high priest kills the bullock (which is his own offering), takes its blood into the Holy of Holies, and sprinkles it on and before the mercy seat. Coming out again, he kills the goat (the people's sin offering) and takes its blood into the Holy of Holies, performing the same ritual acts toward the mercy seat. Next, blood is applied to the Tabernacle and to the horns of the altar, the whole ceremony being designed to make an expiation for the high priest himself, for the people, and for every part of the sanctuary where God's presence was manifested. However these actions are to be explained, the assumption is clear that through the blood of the appointed victims all the deterrents and hindrances to a full and free communion between God and his people could be removed. Every year a new beginning was made possible through the ritual acts which the high priest performed.

Today we are naturally inclined to ask why anyone could ever have thought that such strange ritual actions could achieve such remarkable results. But no direct answer to this question can be given. It is evident that in the Day of Atonement ceremonial there was a complicated elaboration of something that had for centuries been a regular feature of sacrifice, namely, the manipulation of the blood of the victim by the priest. Moreover, we have a valuable hint in Lev. 17:11 ff. to the effect that blood was regarded as the very seat of life and therefore as peculiarly sacred. When blood was sprinkled or applied, it was assumed, apparently, that old stains or defilements or deteriorations were covered up and annulled and that healthy life was now able to circulate afresh without let or hindrance. In the far distant past there may have been the instinctive belief that when life was taken from the earth or from the animal creation the essence of life must be restored to it. Thus through blood, the seat of life, a due return was made to the deity from whom life had been taken. Be that as it may, the ceremonies as we find them in Lev., ch. 16, simply assume that the priest had to manipulate the blood in the prescribed manner in order that a general purgation might be effected and proper relationships restored. Then in Heb., ch. 9, we find the writer taking over this general assumption and using it to interpret to his readers the meaning of the supreme action which the great High Priest had performed when he had taken the blood of his own sacrifice into the immediate presence of God.

The comparison set forth in Heb., ch. 9, is vivid and impressive. The Aaronic high priest exercised his ministry in an earthly tabernacle; Christ exercises his ministry in a tabernacle not made with hands. The high priest performed ceremonial acts in which he used the blood of bulls and goats; Christ by his own blood entered once for all into the sanctuary of God. If, then, the blood of animals sanctifies to the purifying of the flesh, " how much more shall the blood of Christ, who through the eternal Spirit offered himself without spot to God, purge your consciences from dead works to serve the living God? " The contrast is complete: on the one side an act periodically repeated, within an earthly sanctuary, using the blood of animal victims, and having as its purpose the cleansing of outward objects; on the other side an act performed once for all, within a heavenly sanctuary, through the blood of the divine Son of God, and having as its purpose the cleansing of the inner conscience, so that men might be brought into living fellowship with God.

"The blood of Jesus Christ his Son," says the Johannine writer, "goes on cleansing us from all sin." However little the imagery of The Epistle to the Hebrews may appeal to us today, this is the essential message that it proclaims. Just as the application of blood by the priest in ancient rituals was regarded as the means of keeping open the channels between God and man, of maintaining the constant life flow between God and his created order, so in the Christian economy it is the life of Christ, poured out in death and taken again, that breaks down the pride and banishes the selfishness which keep men from God. Or to put it another way, just as through beholding the ancient Greek tragedies men's souls were purified through pity and terror, so when men see the Son of God resisting even unto blood, when they see the blood and water flowing from his pierced side, when they see him making peace through the blood of his cross, then their consciences are convicted and shamed while at the same time their hopes are revived — the blood of Christ purges from dead works to serve the living God. There is here nothing of magic. The image is realistic but not crude. Christ, our great High Priest, through the virtue of his blood-shedding, goes on mediating to his people the inner spirit of his sacrifice and thereby brings them unashamed into the most holy presence of God.

The second Old Testament scene to which the writer of The Epistle to the Hebrews appeals in his ninth chapter is that recorded in Ex., ch. 24. Through a series of dramatic ritual actions the covenant is inaugurated between God and his people. At the center of the picture stands Moses, and to all intents and purposes he plays the part of the priest in the ceremony. Burnt offerings and peace offerings are slain and the blood is collected into basins. Then half of the blood is sprinkled on the altar (almost certainly the symbol of God's own presence) and the other half over the people. In solemn words Moses then declares, "Behold the blood of the covenant, which the Lord hath made with you."

Thus, as the writer of The Epistle to the Hebrews points out, the covenant was dedicated with blood, and a type was thereby provided of a greater covenant which would be sealed by the blood of the covenant maker himself. Actually he does not elaborate the idea further in this chapter, partly because he returns to the imagery of the Day of Atonement for other lessons. But in two other passages in the Epistle he refers to the " blood of the covenant," once in ch. 10:29, when he significantly defines a Christian as a man who has been hallowed by being brought into covenant relationship with God through Christ, and again in ch. 13:20, when Jesus' resurrection is regarded as leading to the establishment of a new covenant through his blood. In this case the blood is conceived as the continuing energy through which he works. As Westcott finely says, " When He was brought up from the dead, the power of his life offered for the world was, as it were, the atmosphere which surrounded him as he entered on his triumphant work."

But although it would be unsafe to infer too much from the references to covenant blood in The Epistle to the Hebrews, the records of the institution of the Lord's Supper as given in the Synoptic Gospels and in I Cor., ch. 11, are such as to leave us in no doubt about the importance of this symbolism in Christian life and experience. According to the records, Jesus, on the night in which he was betrayed, took a cup of wine and constituted it the seal of the new covenant in his blood. Just as the old covenant at Sinai was established through the blood of animals being applied both to God's altar and to the people, so now the new covenant is established through the blood of the Messiah being symbolically shared by the new Israel of God. In ancient times a covenant was sealed by a literal sharing of blood; sometimes the participants drank one another's blood, sometimes arms were slit and pressed together in a common flow of blood. In sharing blood, the seat of life, the two parties were irrevocably bound together in a common existence. The form of expression has changed but the basic idea remains unaltered. Now in the Christian Church, when we receive the wine which is the sacrament of His life outpoured in sacrifice, we come to dwell in him and he in us. He, the great High Priest, binds his people to God and to one another through bringing them within the operation of the eternal covenant sealed forever by his blood.

We have sought to touch briefly upon the main examples of the use of the blood symbol in the New Testament. It has proved to be one of the most powerful symbols in Christian history, partly because it draws upon some of the oldest experiences of the human race, partly because it dramatically and effectively recalls the circumstances of Christ's own death. We may sum up the New Testament evidence by saying, first, that this symbol bears witness to the utter *costliness* of Christ's death: we were redeemed, not with silver and gold, but with precious blood. Secondly, it bears witness to the profound spiritual *efficacy* of Christ's death: Our consciences were purified, not with the blood of bulls and goats, but with the blood of Christ. Thirdly, it bears witness to the intense *purposiveness* of Christ's death: he bound us to himself and to his Father, not with the bonds of a law of contract, but with his own lifeblood, thus making us his forever through the blood of the eternal covenant. In two of the most beautiful phrases of the New Testament: He " made peace through the blood of his cross." " Ye who sometime were far off are made nigh by the blood of Christ."

" Lo, I Come to Do Thy Will "

We have suggested that the second main part of the priest's function in the sacrificial ritual was the actual dedication of the whole offering or of a significant part of it to the deity. In the simplest kind of sacrifice, the offering of the first fruits, the priest took the basket from the offerer's hands and solemnly set it down before the altar of God. In the more complex forms of animal sacrifice, the priest carried out the rules according to the particular type of offering, sometimes setting part of the victim on the altar and sometimes allowing the whole carcass to be consumed by the fire. How far, then, is this function of the priest used by the New Testament writers to describe the work of Christ?

In the Synoptic Gospels, it is again in the narratives of the institution of the Lord's Supper that we may see the clearest references. " And as they did eat, Jesus took bread, and *blessed,* and brake it, and gave to them, and said, Take, eat; this is my body." The body is dedicated in symbolic form, to be broken and given for the life of men. In the Fourth Gospel, the sacrificial note is more prominent, especially in ch. 6. Jesus there affirms that he gives his flesh for the life of the world. This is the true bread of God, the body of Him who came not to do his own will but the will of Him that sent him. For the sake of his disciples, Jesus deliberately offers himself to be sacrificed " that they might be sanctified through the truth " (ch. 17:19). The Pauline writings seldom make use of this imagery. The only notable example is to be found in Eph. 5:2: " Walk in love, as Christ also hath loved us, and hath given himself for us an offering and a sacrifice to God for a sweet-smelling savor."

Elsewhere Paul speaks of Christ's giving himself up on behalf of men, but here only does he say that in so doing he gave himself as an offering and a sacrifice to God. Elsewhere, too, he speaks of a sweet-smelling savor (II Cor. 2:14-16, of his own missionary life; Phil. 4:18, of the kind generosity of his friends in Philippi), but here only does he employ the phrase (derived from the sacrificial terminology of the Old Testament) to the self-giving of Christ. Perhaps the most interesting phrase in the passage is " an offering and a sacrifice," for it appears to be a direct quotation from Ps. 40:6, to which we shall have cause to refer again shortly. Taken as a whole, the passage provides a vivid picture of the Christ offering a perfect sacrifice to God in and through his outpoured life of love and devotion to his own people.

But it is to The Epistle to the Hebrews that we must turn to find a full exposition of the nature of the offering of Christ. Already in Heb., ch. 5, the author has stressed the fact that it is an essential part of the office of any priest to offer gifts and sacrifices and that part, at least, of Christ's sacrifice was the offering of prayers and supplications with the strong crying and tears which formed so notable a feature of his life. But it is in ch. 10 that the author returns to the theme. He is concerned to show once for all the absolute contrast between the sacrifice of Christ and the Levitical sacrifices which were offered year by year continually. Those sacrifices used the bodies of bulls and goats and were never able to make a real purgation of sins. Suddenly the author turns to a famous passage in the Fortieth Psalm, which he quotes from the Greek version:

> " Sacrifice and offering thou wouldest not,
> But a body hast thou prepared me:
> In burnt offerings and sacrifices
>   for sin thou hast had no pleasure.
> Then said I, Lo, I have come to do thy
>   will, O God,
> As it is written of me in the volume
>   of the book."

This is one of the most remarkable prayers of the Old Testament. Realizing how great have been God's mercies to him, the psalmist asks himself how he can show his gratitude. Not, he decides, by going to the sanctuary and presenting sacrifices and offerings. Rather, he will come with the roll of the book in which God's will has been written and he will solemnly consecrate himself to do that will in every detail. Yes, he will delight to do God's will; he will set it constantly within his heart. Such seems to have been the original force of the psalm.

Now, however, the writer of The Epistle to the Hebrews makes certain significant changes. Mainly these derive from the Greek text of the psalm, which translates the phrase, " Mine ears hast thou opened " — that is, to hear thy law — by the words, " A body hast thou prepared me." The reasons for this change need not detain us, but it meant that our author had a striking phrase ready for application to the Christ: Sacrifice and offering thou didst not desire but thou hast prepared for me a body — and immediately it is seen how aptly this describes the mission of Christ. Not bulls and goats — valuable though that symbolism may have been under certain conditions — but his own body, the body prepared for him by God and the body in which his incarnate life was lived. Through that body he will offer himself to do the will of God. So the author reaches his triumphant conclusion: "By the which will we are sanctified through the offering of the body of Jesus Christ once for all."

We have attempted to elucidate the meaning of certain detailed phrases in the passage but its total meaning is plain. The Old Testament saint had perceived that no merely formal presentation of sacrifices and offerings was acceptable to God. It was necessary for him to present his ears, and indeed his whole mind, to receive the revelation of God's will and then to consecrate himself to the performance of it. In one significant point the writer of the Epistle goes beyond this. Christ, he says, presented his whole body to the doing of the will of God, even to the point of offering that body as a sacrifice well-pleasing to God. Here he joins hands with the writer of the Epistle to the Ephesians who, as we saw earlier, says that in the place of the formal " sacrifice and offering " described by the psalmist, Christ gave himself to God as an altogether fragrant and acceptable " sacrifice and offering." In short, the witness of both writers is that in Christ we see a full, perfect, and sufficient dedication to the will of God, issuing finally in the offering of his body on the altar of the cross once and for all. This High Priest has offered his own body, and it is on the ground of this all-inclusive act that we too may offer our bodies as living sacrifices to do the good and acceptable and perfect will of God (Rom. 12:1, 2).

Possibly no short statement in the New Testament more adequately describes the heart and mind of Jesus than does this, taken from Heb., ch. 10:

> " A body hast thou prepared me: . . .
> Lo, I come to do thy will, O God."

We may imagine that at every stage in his life, and in face of every new experience, this was his prayer. His willingness was not an attitude that could be described as " purely spiritual." Rather, it expressed itself constantly through the body that had been prepared for him. Through his body he was related to his physical and social environment and it was there that God's will had to be done. The holiness of that will had to be made known; the purpose of love had also to be made known. And that finally meant a body offered in love to all that holy judgment might demand. He saved others; himself he could not save.

So by that will, by that acceptance, by that perfect self-offering, we have, in the words of the writer to the Hebrews, been sanctified once for all. Calvary has become the central altar of the ages. Christ has become the great High Priest. The way has been opened for all men to enter into the holy presence of God through the virtue of his body offered in sacrifice, his life poured out in death. In a noble passage J. M. E. Ross expresses the matter thus: " At the last, in the exercise of His power over himself, he stretched himself upon the cross. So he became the world's High Priest, offering the sacrifice for which the ages from Abraham onwards had been searching, for which God had been waiting. So the cross became an altar indeed, strange, rude, repellent, yet never to pass as other altars passed, the one Shrine forever for souls that know their need and their sin " (*The Tree of Healing*, p. 124).

" Take, Eat; This Is My Body "

The third main part of the priest's duty in the sacrificial ceremonial was to distribute to the worshipers the portions of the offering to which they were entitled. All too often in the history of Christian devotion the idea of sacrifice has been surrounded by an aura of tragedy and gloom, but the normal atmosphere of sacrifices in the ancient world was that of thanksgiving and rejoicing. Even the sin offerings and guilt offerings were means of removing hindrances to fellowship, and their climax, consequently, was a renewed sense of well-being. In most cases the final stage of the sacrifice was a Eucharistic meal, in which the worshipers ate and drank in the presence of God.

An interesting example of the sacrificial meal is to be seen in the ritual of the Passover. Though customs seem to have varied at different periods and sometimes the sprinkling of the blood on the doorposts may have occupied the place of greatest prominence in the ritual, yet at all times the meal seems to have been an essential part of the celebration. After its blood had been properly dealt with, the lamb was roasted, and then at evening time the family gathered together for a solemn feast. It was a time of remembrance and thanksgiving, in which those present seemed to be sharing again in the experience of their fathers, who had been delivered from the bondage of Egypt. How far the participants saw any deep significance in the flesh on which they feasted it is impossible to say; probably their chief desire was to repeat the circumstances of the original occasion as faithfully as possible. But at least there was the deep sense that the gifts provided at the feast came from God himself, and that the lamb in particular had been given by him as the means of their redemption.

There can be little doubt that the early Christian practice of the breaking of bread had close associations with the Jewish Passover. In the Synoptic accounts of the institution of the Lord's Supper, special reference is made to the Passover season, and in the Johannine account of the crucifixion it is indicated that Jesus' death took place at the very time when the Passover lambs were being killed. In a striking outburst in I Cor., ch. 5, the apostle Paul, pleading for a radical reform in the community, recalls the Passover season when all old leaven was removed before the festival began. But Christ our passover Lamb has been sacrificed already. Therefore he cries, let us keep our festival, not with old leaven, the leaven of malice and wickedness, but with the unleavened bread of sincerity and truth. His point is that the whole Christian life should be a Passover festival, feeding on the new bread from heaven and unspoiled by unworthy relics of a former existence.

In this new festival existence there was, however, a constantly recurring occasion when their Lord was present in a special way to feed his faithful people with the tokens of his sacrifice. He who had offered his body once for all now drew near to his worshipers, saying, "Take, eat; this is my body." He who had shed his life-blood now held out the cup, saying, "Drink ye all of it." Until men actually partake of his body and blood, the sacrificial action fails to reach its wholeness of expression. "Except ye eat the flesh of the Son of man, and drink his blood, ye have no life in you." But when in thankful adoration men receive at his hands the symbols of his life poured out in death, then fellowship is established and the purpose of the one supreme sacrifice is fulfilled.

In saying this we do not intend to suggest that the sacrificial offering of Christ can be received only at the time when the breaking of bread takes place. Every live coal from off the altar, that is to say, every word, every sign, every action, which has become charged with meaning through its derivation from the blood-shedding and self-offering of Christ himself, can convey to waiting hearts the virtue of his sacrifice. But in a peculiarly appropriate and comprehensive way the Lord's Supper provides the occasion for the great sacrifice to reach its completion in word and deed and for the Lord of the feast to convey to his faithful people the fruits of his redemption. Such is the witness of centuries of Christian devotion. Let us hear, for example, the old monks chanting the lines preserved in the Bangor Antiphonary of the seventh century:

> " Salvation's giver, Christ, the only Son,
>   By His dear cross and blood the victory won.

> " Offered was He for greatest and for least,
>   Himself the Victim and Himself the Priest.

> " Approach ye, then, with faithful hearts sincere
>   And take the pledges of salvation here.

> " He that His saints in this world rules and shields
>   To all believers life eternal yields;

> " With heavenly bread makes them that hunger whole,
>   Gives living waters to the thirsty soul."

Or let us hear the great philosopher of the thirteenth century, Thomas Aquinas, expressing his heart's devotion thus:

" O blest Memorial of our dying Lord,
    Who living Bread to men doth here afford!
    O may our souls for ever feed on Thee,
    And Thou, O Christ, for ever precious be.

" Fountain of goodness, Jesu, Lord and God,
    Cleanse us, unclean, in Thy most cleansing Blood;
    Increase our faith and love, that we may know
    The hope and peace which from Thy Presence flow.

" O Christ, whom now beneath a veil we see,
    May what we thirst for soon our portion be,
    To gaze on Thee unveiled, and see Thy face,
    The vision of Thy glory and Thy grace."

Or, coming nearer to our own day, no hymn writer standing in
the pietist and evangelical tradition has given such a wealth of
Eucharistic hymns to the Church at large as has Charles Wesley.
Let us listen to one that is simple but richly comprehensive:

" Author of life divine,
        Who hast a table spread,
    Furnished with mystic Wine
        And everlasting Bread,
    Preserve the life Thyself hast given,
    And feed and train us up for heaven.

" Our needy souls sustain
        With fresh supplies of love,
    Till all Thy life we gain,
        And all Thy fullness prove,
    And, strengthened by Thy perfect grace,
    Behold without a veil Thy face."

Or finally, within the Reformed tradition, let us hear the words of
the Scottish minister Horatius Bonar written for an ordinary
Communion season in his brother's church:

" Here, O my Lord, I see Thee face to face;
        Here would I touch and handle things unseen;
    Here grasp with firmer hand eternal grace,
        And all my weariness upon Thee lean.

" Here would I feed upon the Bread of God;
    Here drink with Thee the royal Wine of heaven;
  Here would I lay aside each earthly load,
    Here taste afresh the calm of sin forgiven.

" I have no help but Thine; nor do I need
    Another arm save Thine to lean upon;
  It is enough, my Lord, enough indeed;
    My strength is in Thy might, Thy might alone.

" Mine is the sin, but Thine the righteousness;
    Mine is the guilt, but Thine the cleansing Blood.
  Here is my robe, my refuge, and my peace;
    Thy Blood, Thy righteousness, O Lord, my God."

Through all these hymns there breathes the spirit of reality and vitality. Within the context of the sacramental drama the Lord himself has drawn near and offered afresh to men the living bread, the royal wine of heaven. They have received the gifts, their souls have been strengthened, and they have gone on their way rejoicing. In this foretaste of heavenly realities their assurance has been renewed and they have hailed the day when all sacramental experiences will be transcended in the vision face to face.

" O Almighty God, our Heavenly Father, who hast accepted us as thy children in thy beloved Son Jesus Christ our Lord, and dost feed us with the spiritual food of his most precious Body and Blood, giving us the forgiveness of our sins and the promise of everlasting life: We thank and praise thee for these inestimable benefits, and we offer and present unto thee ourselves, our souls and bodies, to be a holy and living sacrifice, which is our reasonable service. Grant us grace not to be conformed to this world, but to be transformed by the renewing of our minds, that we may learn what is thy good and perfect will, and so obey thee here on earth, that we may at the last rejoice with all thy saints in thy Heavenly Kingdom. Through Jesus Christ our Lord, who liveth and reigneth with thee and the Holy Spirit, one God, forever. Amen." — *From the Service of the Lord's Supper*
                    Authorized by the Church of South India.

Chapter VII

THE SERVANT OF THE LORD

"He left His Father's throne above, —
So free, so infinite His grace —
Emptied Himself of all but love,
And bled for Adam's helpless race."

One of the most interesting fields of study in the history of early Christianity is that of the hymnody of the primitive Church. At all times the hymns that people sing tell us much about their religious faith. Are they chiefly praises or lamentations? Are they centered upon God and his mighty acts or upon the soul and its inward experiences? Are they subdued and regular or are they spontaneous and exultant? Hymns not only arise out of faith but they create and sustain faith. They are, therefore, of peculiar significance in that they reveal not only the substance of the faith but also the general outlook of those who hold it. It is important then to ask whether any survivals of the hymns of the apostolic age have been preserved for us in the New Testament.

This is not an easy question to answer, for under the influence of strong emotion men will often speak in a semipoetical way and we cannot always be sure that passages with a balanced and rhythmical structure represent formal hymns. However, there can be little doubt about the songs recorded in the early chapters of Luke's Gospel or about the anthems of the heavenly choirs contained in the book of Revelation. These were almost certainly in use in early Christian circles and they bear witness to the deep gratitude for redemption which animated those who sang them. Of other possible examples of early Christian praise, quite the most interesting is the noble passage contained in Phil. 2:6-11.

Commentators have for long recognized that in their original form in the Greek, these verses possess a rhythm and a balance that put them in the category of poetry rather than of prose.

Various attempts have been made to set out the hymn in its original versification and we shall take one of these as the basis of our examinations of the teaching of the passage. It runs as follows:

"Who, being in the form of God,
 thought it not robbery
  to be equal with God:

"but made himself of no reputation,
 taking upon him the form of a servant,
 and being made in the likeness of men:

"and being found in fashion as a man,
 he humbled himself,
 and became obedient unto death,
  even the death of the cross.

"Wherefore God also hath highly exalted him,
 and given him a name
 which is above every name:

"that at the name of Jesus
 every knee should bow,
 of things in heaven, and things
  in earth, and things under the earth;

"and that every tongue should confess
 that Jesus Christ is Lord,
 to the glory of God the Father."

As can easily be seen, the first three stanzas describe the humiliation of Christ Jesus; the second three, his exaltation. The first three might be entitled "The Form of a Servant"; the second three, "Jesus Christ Is Lord." The whole poem might bear the title of this book: "*Jesus Christ and His Cross.*" The only serious break in the structure is at the end of the third stanza, where an extra line seems to have been added. If it could be assumed that the apostle was quoting a hymn already in use in the Church, how appropriate it would seem that he himself should have added as a comment or as an aside: " even the death of the cross " ! No one could have stooped lower than the Saviour did; no one can ever be exalted so high as he, for at his name *every* knee shall bow.

When we begin to examine the poem more carefully, we find ourselves recalling two Old Testament passages in which similar phrases and ideas occur. We think first of the narrative of Gen., chs. 1 to 3. Here we read of a man created in the image and likeness of God and given dominion over every living creature. Yet when the tempter whispered the suggestion that by disobeying the command of God he might exalt himself to the place where " ye shall be as gods, knowing good and evil," he took the way of disobedience and ate the fruit of the tree. So the first Adam lost his fair estate. He became subject to toil and sweat and the curse of the earth, subject to the attacks of the powers of evil, subject to banishment from the paradise of God, subject to the ravages of internecine strife. The story of the first Adam was " From Exaltation to Humiliation by Way of Disobedience." Only in the Second Adam was the downward process reversed and a new humanity restored.

But there is another Old Testament passage that immediately springs to mind. In the last of the Servant Songs (Isa. 52:13 to 53:12) there are phrases that are directly echoed, if not repeated, in the hymn of Phil., ch. 2. " God also hath highly exalted him," " he humbled himself," " obedient unto death," he " made himself of no reputation " — all these phrases in the Greek version of the hymn can be paralleled in Isaiah. Thus it seems almost certain that the writer of the hymn had the Song of the Suffering Servant also in his mind and saw in Christ Jesus not only the antitype of Adam but also the fulfillment of the character typified by Isaiah's Servant. It was through pouring himself out and becoming obedient even to death that the Servant of the Lord was able to justify many and to bear their iniquities. Now he has been exalted and extolled and made very high " and the pleasure of the Lord shall prosper in his hand."

He Made Himself of No Reputation

The beautiful translation of the King James Version does not fully represent the force of the original, though, as we shall see, the mission of the incarnate Son did involve a real share in the disrepute and the shame of mankind. But the more literal translation would be " he emptied himself," " he poured himself out," the same word being used in the Greek version of Isa. 53:12 that is translated " he hath poured out his soul unto death." Rather than snatch for a prize in the manner of Adam, he poured himself out; rather than puff himself up, in the manner of Lucifer, son of the morning, he emptied himself. The self-humbling of majesty, the condescension of deity, was the cause of never-ending wonder to the men of the New Testament.

But what did the self-emptying involve? It certainly involved the pouring of himself into a body of flesh and blood. Inasmuch as those whom he purposed to save were partakers of flesh and blood, he himself partook of the same and thereby exposed himself to the handicaps and limitations which this form of existence necessarily involved. Having poured himself into a human body, he found himself subject to a narrow confinement in space, as well as to a constricted period of time. He could not escape the conditions of a certain environment, nor could he divest himself of the traditions belonging to a certain section of society. He had poured himself into a vessel ready to receive him but also ready to enclose him.

For what did it mean that he was born as a Palestinian Jew, in the days when Caesar Augustus was emperor in Rome and Quirinius was governor of Syria? It meant that he might have lived and died as a child of his age, zealous for the Jewish law, devoted to Jewish institutions, proud of Jewish traditions, eager to promote Jewish aspirations. By this means he could have gained a noble reputation as an Israelite indeed, in whom was no guile. But this would have been to compass himself around by a wall of racial security, to enclose himself within a mold of social approbation. And the principle of his life was to pour himself out.

So it was that although he was constantly being tempted to conform, to submit completely to the standards of the particular society into which he had been born, he steadfastly refused to do so. He could not accept the relative security which would have been his as a 100 per cent Jew. He must pour himself out.

How, then, was this effected? In the first instance, it would seem, by identifying himself with those who went forth to the Jordan to be baptized by John. Here was a movement that was critical of the accepted standards of the day. It did not allow that all was right with the state of Jewry. It did not even allow that a faithful observance of the law and a sincere upholding of religious tradition was enough. The call was to repentance, to turn the back upon human securities and achievements and to cast oneself upon the mercy of God alone. And Jesus joined the repentant Israelites on Jordan's banks and made himself of no reputation as he went down into the stream.

Such an action was bound to be misunderstood. Did it mean that there was some consciousness of inward sin of which he needed to repent? Or did it at least mean that he was conscious of frailty and weakness and liability to sin? There is no necessity to entertain such ideas. If the very keynote of his mission was that of pouring himself out, then nothing could have been more natural than that he should have identified himself with those who were seeking a deeper righteousness than the legal righteousness of their own time, who were looking for a holier kingdom than the restored national kingdom of Israel. It seemed to outward observation to be a contracting vessel into which he was pouring his life and yet in reality it was one that was capable of an ever widening expansion. It was less bound to a particular time and place, though it was not yet free enough to become the society of universal range. For the time being, Jesus remained within the circle of John's mission, but even that soon became too constricted an environment. Perhaps the pattern of the movement crystallized too firmly within the moralistic demands and the sacramental requirements which John imposed. What is clear is that Jesus did not continue indefinitely in the company of those with whom he had identified himself, but instead went forth to his own special vocation in which he was to pour himself out still further.

The unanimous testimony of the Gospel records is that he "made himself of no reputation" by deliberately choosing to identify himself with the publicans and the sinners, the poor and the outcast. No scene more vividly portrays the manner of Jesus' outpouring and the resultant reaction than that which is recorded in Luke 4: 16-30. Here we read that upon a certain Sabbath Day Jesus went into the Nazareth synagogue and announced the character of his mission:

"The Spirit of the Lord is upon me, because he hath anointed me to preach the gospel to the poor; he hath sent me to heal the broken-hearted, to preach deliverance to the captives, and recovering of sight to the blind, to set at liberty them that are bruised, to preach the acceptable year of the Lord."

The poor, the captives, the brokenhearted, the blind, the bruised — in soul as well as body! But people of this kind are to be found not only in the particular country of Israel. Elijah was sent to a poor widow in Sidon; Elisha brought succor to an afflicted leper from Syria. These classes of people are to be found in *every* place, at *every* period of time, and it is with these that Jesus now identifies himself. He will make common cause with the despised and the rejected, the sick and the lost. He will pour himself out and make himself of no reputation so that he may be with them just where they are. Let them be Jew or Gentile, bond or free, male or female — if they need one to serve them and to save them, he will be there, pouring himself out and proclaiming the acceptable year of the Lord.

But there is one further step in identification — the hardest and loneliest of all. In the remarkable account that Luke gives of the events at the supper table on the night of Jesus' betrayal, there are two significant scenes that immediately precede the departure to the Garden. In one of these, the disciples may be seen still arguing and striving with one another about places of precedence in the coming Kingdom. Jesus' rebuke is couched in terms of service. The highest dignity is to be the servant: "I am among you as he that serveth." The servant of the Lord has no thought of grasping for the place of privilege; to the end he will continue in the role of the servant. In the second scene it is Peter who may be seen bravely protesting that he is willing to go with Jesus even to prison and to death. But Jesus knows that only after he has passed through a fire of testing will he be able to lead and strengthen his brethren. Meanwhile, as the scene draws toward its close, Jesus declares that a final portion of the Servant's destiny has yet to be fulfilled in his own career: " And he was numbered with the transgressors." So they all depart to the Mount of Olives.

But this is not the only reference to this particular saying in the Gospel narratives. In Mark's account of the crucifixion the record reads thus:

" And the superscription of his accusation was written over, THE KING OF THE JEWS.

" And with him they crucify two thieves; the one on his right hand, and the other on his left.

" And the Scripture was fulfilled, which saith, And he was numbered with the transgressors."

This is the final shame, the final indignity, the final self-emptying: on the cross, between two others who had been condemned to death as unworthy of continuing any longer in the life of the community, Jesus was regarded as a common felon, a menace to society, a man worthy only of a place among criminals. So he reached the final stage of his outpouring. He could step no lower: he was making his grave with the wicked and suffering the shame of the death of a transgressor.

As we ponder these successive stages of self-emptying, we are reminded of one figure from the Old Testament who in a wonderful way entered already into something of the Servant's experience. The early stages are described by the writer of The Epistle to the Hebrews in imperishable words:

" By faith Moses, when he was come to years, refused to be called the son of Pharaoh's daughter;

" Choosing rather to suffer affliction with the people of God, than to enjoy the pleasures of sin for a season;

"Esteeming the reproach of Christ greater riches than the treasures in Egypt: for he had respect unto the recompense of the reward."

He might have grown up in the court of Egypt and attained a position of highest eminence in the imperial regime. Instead, he deliberately took the part of the slave laborers and went into exile for his pains. Returning, he identified himself still more deeply with them, became their representative and their champion, and thereby stood in the eyes of the Egyptians as no more than an abomination. Going forth from Egypt, he committed himself to the even more difficult task of bearing with the undisciplined horde in their weaknesses, their murmurings, their backslidings. Finally, in one significant incident, the process of self-emptying reached its climax. During a period of Moses' absence in the Mount the people had apostatized to the extent of making a golden calf, offering sacrifices to it, feasting before it, and indulging in primitive orgies of dance and song. What will he do? Will Moses still identify himself with them? In one of the noblest prayers ever framed Moses cries to the Lord: "Oh, this people have sinned a great sin, and have made them gods of gold. Yet now, if thou wilt forgive their sin — ; and if not, blot me, I pray thee, out of thy book which thou hast written." Perhaps nowhere in the whole historical experience of mankind do we come nearer to the spirit of Calvary than at this place. Moses numbered himself with the transgressors; he identified himself with the lost; he poured out his soul for his people.

But it was the constant ministry of Jesus to be *pouring* himself out. Horace Bushnell, in one of his letters, tells of his third visit to Niagara Falls. Never had he been so impressed before. True, he says, it is only a magnificent, mechanical "pour off one higher shelf" of the world upon another that is lower. But "it is so great in itself, and magnifies so wonderfully the revelation of its grandeur, that it finally conquers, and compels us at last to say, 'There is nothing like it, nothing of magnificence to class with it.' Oh, this pouring on, on, on — exhaustless, ceaseless, like the counsel itself of God — one ocean plunging in solemn repose of continuity into another; the breadth, the height, the volume, the absence of all fluster, as when the floods lift up their waves; the self-confidence of the preparation, as grand in the night when no eye sees it as in the day; still bending itself downward to the plunge, as a power that is the same yesterday, today, and forever; wanting no margin of attractions to complement the scene it makes; making, in fact, no scene, but doing a *deed* which is enough to do, whether it is seen or not! " It is a fascinating thought that of all the natural phenomena of the world the most majestic and most impressive may be the greatest scene of *outpouring* known to man. Certain it is that within the divine economy nothing compares in significance with the outpouring by which the Son of God made himself of no reputation and was numbered with the transgressors.

The Form of a Servant

We have spoken of the process by which he who was in the form of God emptied himself out until he took his place with the lowest of mankind. But in the course of this process there was one role that he was always fulfilling — he was a *servant*. Whatever one's position or status in life, it is possible to be a servant. This has been in a measure perceived by the princes of the Church or of the State who have from time to time made public pronouncement to the effect that it is their highest aim to be the *servants* of the people. But in the case of Jesus this was the role that he was determined to fulfill consistently and unceasingly. Nowhere is this whole tenor of his life more beautifully expressed than in the acted parable recorded for us in John 13:1-17. The tiny drama of the washing of the disciples' feet may well be regarded as an expansion and an exposition of the Pauline phrase, " the form of a servant."

As soon as we examine the narrative, we find that it bears marked resemblances to a drama. There is a solemn prologue and a telling epilogue. The scene itself is a compound of words and actions full of surprise and dramatic intensity; we cannot escape the feeling that there are depths of meaning that do not appear on the surface of the recorded events. The prologue reveals the true dignity of the chief actor in the drama: he came from God and went to God and the Father had given all things into his hands. It also reveals his essential character: having loved, he loved to the very limit, completely and finally, to the uttermost, unto death; he held nothing back, as the ensuing scene is to show. So the drama begins to unfold. Jesus rises from supper — and there is the sense that something of unusual importance is pending; he lays aside his garments — the marks of status and dignity — and girds himself with a towel, the mark of the bondslave. He pours water into a basin — and although the word is not the same as that used for self-emptying in Phil. 2:7 the idea is closely akin — and he begins to wash the disciples' feet — the most menial form of service that one man could render to another. As Clement of Alexandria so beautifully says: " The Lord ate from a cheap bowl, and he washed his disciples' feet with a towel about him — the lowly-minded God and Lord of the universe. He did not bring a silver footbath from heaven to carry about with him." He who came from God and went to God declares by this parable that to stoop is to conquer, to serve is to reign.

Let us now mark certain characteristics of this career of service:

1. The most obvious feature of the work of a slave, at all periods of human history, has been his duty to do the *dirty* work of society, to perform tasks that the ordinary person finds distasteful and even revolting. Whether it be the cleansing of the traveler's feet, or the disposal of excrement and garbage, or the removal of the grime that gathers on walls and buildings; whether it be the washing of soiled linen or the sweeping of the dusty room, all are tasks that have no attraction in themselves. They are necessary for the well-being of society and carry with them a certain promise of satisfaction when the work is well done. But few would choose to spend their lives doing the dirty work of the community if they could help it and one of the most notable advances of modern man has come about through his ability to construct machinery that will do much of his dirty work for him. At the same time there is little immediate prospect of machinery's being multiplied

to such an extent that the vast labor of removing dirt can be performed by any other agency than man himself. Someone must still be prepared to deal with the world's filth and refuse.

In a penetrating essay on the general subject of "Dirt," the late Edwyn Bevan showed that in a strange way all man's deepest feelings of horror and repulsion are associated with dirt that is in some way related to the human *body*. Mud on a side road, tar in a barrel, coal dust in the air — these become definitely offensive to us only if they have become in some way attached to our bodies. Decaying material revolts us when its stench enters our lungs. Clothes repel us when they have been soiled by any form of excrement from the human body. As Bevan says: "Deep at the bottom of all our sense of uncleanliness, of dirt, is the feeling, primitive, irresolvable, universal, of the sanctity of the body. Nothing in the material sphere can be properly dirty except the body." And the consequence is that anyone handling the dirt of the body becomes in a certain sense unclean himself. He must at least submit to thorough purification before he can be readmitted to a normal existence within the society to which he desires to belong.

To say that all this is irrational and absurd does not alter these instincts which are deeply ingrained in human nature. It may be irrational to say that mud on the body is any different from mud on the public pathway, but the fact remains that man *feels* it is different and by so doing guards the sanctity of his body in a symbolic way. If distinctions of this kind are irrelevant, then the body itself is of no account and may be manipulated and used just like any other piece of matter. But if there is a certain sanctity attaching to the body; if, in other words, our bodies are not the property of ourselves or of anyone else but belong in the last resort to God; if, in some way, our bodies are temples of the Holy Spirit, then the body must be preserved from defilement by any elements of dead or decaying matter. If that which is inert or lifeless is allowed to remain in permanent contact with the body, the body is prevented from fulfilling its function as the shrine of the living Spirit of God. To cleanse the body is to fulfill a task of a sacramental kind. Those who perform the task in any way, though they may need to be cleansed themselves from the impurities they have contracted, yet deserve to be regarded as among the highest benefactors of mankind.

But there is one further thing to be said. If, as the Hebrews believed and as is being more and more emphasized in modern theory, body and soul are mutually related to one another, then dirt on the body cannot be wholly separate from dirt on the soul; cleansing of the one is intimately related to cleansing of the other. Not that a merely outward cleansing can purify the inner springs of the personality; nor can a formal absolution cleanse the body from its defilements. But even a refreshing bath can bring about a new sense of general well-being and the removal of a guilt complex can soon show its effects in bodily healing. These interconnections are exceedingly delicate and mysterious but they are clear enough to enhance our vision of the One who, taking upon himself the form of a servant and sharing the great task of outward cleansing, revealed himself as the purifier of the whole man, the one who by his sacrificial activity cleanses man from all defilement. If the task of removing outward impurities is hard and menial and often contemptible, how much harder is the task of removing the dirt of the soul! The confessor and the confidant, the psychiatrist and the social worker — all are compelled to listen to and in a measure to handle the filth and the refuse of human souls. The more sensitive their own faculties, the more painful will their task become. And how could the task of the Servant of the Lord, who received upon his own soul the whole defilement of the human race, have been other than agony and distress beyond our conceiving? The New Testament says, and the testimony of the Church has said, that cleansing is only through his blood. He who washed the disciples' feet with water washed their souls with blood. He who shared the dirty work of the body undertook the most sordid work of the soul. Again, this may not yield to rational explanation but it somehow speaks to the deepest needs of the soul.

2. The second distinctive feature of the work of a slave has

been his duty to perform the *heavy* work of society, to undertake those tasks which the ordinary person finds burdensome and even killing. The records of slave gangs carrying building materials for their imperial overlords are well known. But even in modern times no one who has seen a coolie porter carrying mountains of baggage on his back at an Indian port or a rough hillman being weighed down by a gigantic basket of charcoal on a narrow pathway in the Himalayas will ever have any illusions about what it means to be a slave in a society where no animals are available and machinery has not yet been set up to do the heavy work of mankind.

The burdens that have to be borne are normally those connected with man's everyday needs. It is true that when cities grow and ambitious building programs are conceived, much carrying has to be done that cannot be regarded as essential in the very nature of things. But however simply a society may be organized, water has to be carried from the stream or well, fuel has to be carried for the fire, and food has to be brought from forest or field. For some reason, those who have been responsible for bearing these burdens have rarely been honored or appreciated. Perhaps because the work has involved strain and drudgery, perhaps because those who bear burdens are weighted down and have the appearance of being oppressed, there has been a tendency to despise and contemn the man or woman who does the heavy work. Yet if this task is an essential part of the basic organization of life, it should clearly be given a high place of honor in a society's scale of values. At few places can value judgments have been more distorted than at the point where the worth of the servant who does the dirty work and bears the heavy burdens is estimated. Usually there has been little reward given to those who have borne the burden and heat of the day, to those who have done the unspectacular things, to those who have kept life going by a faithful shouldering of commonplace duties. They have been the *servants,* and the servant has had " no form nor comeliness " and there has been little beauty in his task.

The same connection exists between body and soul in this area as in the area of the cleansing of defilement. Burdens of the body all too easily cause a dull and heavy mind; heavy personal anxieties constantly cause disease and bodily disorder. The servant who bears a heavy physical burden makes it possible for others to enjoy a greater freedom for the expansion of their souls; the servant of the community who invites heavy-laden souls to roll off their mental burdens onto his shoulders, makes it possible for them to discover a new health and integration of their whole personalities. There is nothing inherently degrading in bearing a burden; the degradation comes only when the laborer is forced to bend beneath a dull, mechanical, meaningless load, day after day, without a ray of hope of change or relief in the future. Similarly, in the life of the mind or spirit there is nothing noble or honorable in being free of or superior to the burdens of ordinary humanity. It is strange that some of the great writers of our day, viewing the frailties and follies of their contemporaries, seeing man as a creature weighed down by the lusts and cravings of the flesh, perceiving the emergence of mass man (a term that hauntingly suggests the dull, weary weight of human existence) with all his potentialities for evil, can do little more than pour contempt upon the human race and ridicule upon the human scene. It has been said that the essential message of one of the greatest dramatists of our day may be summarized thus: " The world is futile and so are its inhabitants. Let us therefore drink ourselves to death if we have not enough courage to blow out our brains." On the other hand, whereas such a play as *The Cocktail Party* does not hesitate to expose the dull round of existence which marks so much of contemporary life, there may be felt running through it a note, not of contempt, but rather of compassion. Even through his play the author seeks to bear something of the boredom and meaninglessness of bourgeois existence and to suggest ever so delicately a way of release.

The Servant of the Lord, in a way that none other has ever done, chooses to be the burden bearer of the sins and sorrows of mankind. This was the theme that Horace Bushnell made it his aim to expound in his great work " The Vicarious Sacrifice."

Unsatisfied with the treatments of the doctrine of the atonement current in his day, he deliberately chose the word " vicarious " as the one best fitted to express the nature of the work of Christ. Before long it becomes clear that the principle of vicariousness is none other than the principle of love " and it is the nature of love universally, to insert itself into the miseries and take upon its feeling the burdens of others. Love does not consider the ill desert of the subject; he may even be a cruel and relentless enemy. It does not consider the expense of toil, and sacrifice, and suffering the intervention may cost. It stops at nothing but the known impossibility of relief or benefit; asks for nothing as inducement but the opportunity of success. Love is a principle essentially vicarious in its own nature, identifying the subject with others, so as to suffer their adversities and pains, and taking on itself the burden of their evils." Bushnell dwells on the Matthaean application of " Himself took our infirmities, and bare our sicknesses " to the ministry of Jesus. What does it mean? " Does it mean that he literally had our sicknesses transferred to him and so taken off from us? Does it mean that he became blind for the blind, lame for the lame, a leper for the lepers, suffering in himself all the fevers and pains that he took away from others? No one had ever such a thought. How, then, did he bear our sicknesses, or in what sense? In the sense that he took them on his feeling, had his heart burdened by the sense of them, bore the disgusts of their loathsome decays, felt their pains over again, in the tenderness of his more than human sensibility." In the very same way, the bearing of our sins means " that Christ bore them on his feeling, became inserted into their bad lot by his sympathy as a friend, yielded up himself and his life, even, to an effort of restoring mercy; in a word, that he bore our sins in just the same sense that he bore our sicknesses." Love is " an essentially vicarious principle." To understand in the smallest measure the meaning of a love which goes into action by bearing the burdens of others is to begin to penetrate to the heart of the mystery of the cross.

"I Have Given You an Example"

The New Testament nowhere provides a collection of detailed rules to guide the disciple every step of his way. It does not attempt to show how he is to behave in every imaginable set of circumstances. Instead, it sets before us the One who entered history in the form of a servant, and by telling the story of Jesus — his baptism, his temptation, his preaching, his works of healing, his prayers, his attitude to the outcasts of society, his relations to his disciples, his relations to the religious and political authorities of his time, his passion, his death, his exaltation — it gives the all-sufficient example by which the disciple is to live. " Let this mind be in you, which was also in Christ Jesus," it says; " I have given you an example, that ye should do as I have done to you."

It is a remarkable fact that the three passages in the New Testament that speak most fully about the example given to Christian disciples all focus attention upon Christ the *Servant* of the Lord. Two of these (Phil. 2:5-11; John 13:1-17) we have examined already in the course of this chapter. The third is to be found in I Peter 2: 18-25. Here also the portrait of Christ is that taken from Isa., ch. 53. It has been suggested that vs. 21-25 are part of an early Christian hymn, and if this were so, it would show how central in primitive Christian hymnody was the theme of the humiliation and subsequent exaltation of Christ.

> " [Christ] did no sin, neither was
> guile found in his mouth:
> Who, when he was reviled, reviled
> not again; when he suffered,
> he threatened not; but committed
> himself to him that judgeth
> righteously.
> Who his own self bare our sins
> in his own body on the tree."

This is the picture of the Servant of the Lord, and it is in the light of this picture that the Christian disciple is bidden to walk. Christ left us " an example, that ye should follow his steps."

The word used in the passage for " example " is a most interesting one. This is its only occurrence in the New Testament, but in the wider Greek world it stood for one of two things: it might mean the tracing by which children could guide their pens and so gradually form their letters; or it might mean the artist's sketch of a building or the model which needed to be filled in by others. In either case the word represents an outline sketch, not complete in all its details but sufficient in its general form to enable others to proceed with confidence in their task of bringing to concrete expression the example provided for them. This surely suggests a wonderful and most satisfying pattern of Christian living. We are not left without guidance, and yet we are not bound by a rigid code; we are not divested of all responsibility, and yet we are given a rich freedom. In His service (could this be interpreted as " in following the example of the Servant " ?) there is perfect freedom.

It only remains to notice that the Christian disciple will most closely follow the example as he performs the twofold task to which we have already referred — washing the feet of others and bearing their heavy burdens. Amidst all that is uncertain today about the Christian's duty — in international affairs, in the sphere of politics, in the economic order — about one thing there can be no question. The Christian who refuses to undertake the unpleasant and unsavory and even revolting task in any area of life is simply denying his Christian vocation. Nowhere has the true spirit of Christian discipleship been more powerfully illustrated than in the ministry to the lepers of India or Africa or the islands of the Pacific; or than in the rescue work among the slum dwellers of London or Chicago or Tokyo or Cairo; or than in the rehabilitation of battle-torn areas; or than in the struggle on the field of politics with the unclean forces of prejudice and greed and lust and tyranny; or than in the attempt to cleanse the dark corners of perverted and diseased minds. These are outstanding examples of a readiness to pour water into a bowl and to cleanse away the stains of the world. But wherever the humblest disciple in the spirit of the Master washes another's wound and bears witness to the sacrificial blood of Christ in relation to another's sin, there the true nature of Christian service is being revealed, the true meaning of Christian charity is being disclosed.

" Bear ye one another's burdens, and so fulfil the law of Christ " (Gal. 6:2). This is the second aspect of the service of Christ. It is no arbitrary duty imposed upon the disciple. The disciple undertakes it only because he desires to follow in the steps of Him who above all else was and is the burden bearer. If any man had the right to speak on the meaning of Christian discipleship it was the German pastor, Dietrich Bonhoeffer, who determined at all costs to identify himself with his people and yet resisted National Socialism to the bitter end. Ultimately put to death by the SS Black Guards in April, 1945, he had all through the years been ready for sacrifice, and in prison his highest concern had been to minister to the sick and to his fellow prisoners and to comfort the anxious and depressed. What was the secret of this life which has won the admiration of Christian people in many lands? May we not find it in the words that occur toward the end of his meditation on " Discipleship and the Cross " ? " God," he writes, " is a God who *bears*. The Son of God bore our flesh, he bore the cross, he bore our sins, thus making atonement for us. In the same way his followers are also called upon to bear, and that is precisely what it means to be a Christian. Just as Christ maintained his communion with the Father by his endurance, so his followers are to maintain their communion with Christ by their endurance. We can of course shake off the burden which is laid upon us, but only find that we have a still heavier burden to carry — a yoke of our own choosing, the yoke of our self. But Jesus invites all who travail and are heavy-laden to throw off their own yoke and take his yoke upon them — and his yoke is easy, and his burden is light. The yoke and the burden of Christ are his cross."

Bonhoeffer and noble souls like him have carried the burdens of their fellow men openly and dramatically, without indeed seeking the admiration of others, yet forced by the circumstances under which they have lived to stand forth as heroic champions of the afflicted and oppressed. Not to many, however, does the

call come to service on the open plane of public events. Usually
burdens have to be borne silently and even secretly, but the one
who so bears them is equally near to the spirit and succor of the
Christ. One of the most beautiful portrayals of this aspect of
Christian discipleship is to be found in an old devotional classic,
The Spirit of Discipline, by Bishop Francis Paget. The chapter
entitled " The Responsibility of Strength " is based on the verse,
" We then that are strong ought to bear the infirmities of the
weak " (Rom. 15:1). What is the inner meaning of this injunction?
It is, says the writer, " that the strong, in whatsoever sphere their
strength may lie, should try in silence and simplicity, escaping
the observation of men, to take upon their own shoulders the
burdens which the weak are bearing; to submit themselves to the
difficulties amidst which the weak are stumbling; to be, for their
help's sake, as they are, to share the fear, the dimness, the anxiety,
the trouble and heart-sinking through which they have to work
their way; to forgo and lay aside the privilege of strength in order
to understand the weak and backward and bewildered, in order
to be with them, to enter into their thoughts, to wait on their
advance; to be content, if they can only serve, so to speak, as a
favorable circumstance for growth towards that which God intended them to be. It is the innermost reality of sympathy, it is
the very heart and life of courtesy, that is touched here: but like
all that is best in moral beauty, it loses almost all its grace the
moment it attracts attention. It is noblest when it is least conscious, when another's load, another's limitations, another's trials
are assumed quite naturally, as a mother takes her children's
troubles for her own, by the straightforward instinct of her love;
it is impaired whenever the disfiguring shadow of self-conscious-
ness has begun to creep about it; it is ruined utterly, it ceases to
have any semblance of its former self, when once it has been
tainted by any insolent complacency in condescension. But when
it is pure and true and self-forgetful; when it is guarded by a real
hatred of praise, a real joy in hiddenness; when it has no motive
and no goal save love — then, indeed, it may be the distinctive

glory of the Christian character." " I have given you an example, that ye should do as I have done to you."

" Almighty and everlasting God, who, of thy tender love towards mankind, hast sent thy Son, our Saviour Jesus Christ, to take upon him our flesh, and to suffer death upon the cross, that all mankind should follow the example of his great humility; Mercifully grant, that we may both follow the example of his patience, and also be made partakers of his resurrection; through the same Jesus Christ our Lord. Amen." — *Collect for Palm Sunday,* Book of Common Prayer.

Chapter VIII

THE GLORY OF THE CROSS

"In the cross of Christ I glory,
 Towering o'er the wrecks of time;
All the light of sacred story
 Gathers round its head sublime."

————————

"My sinful self my only shame,
 My glory all, the cross."

There is a dramatic scene, recorded only in the Fourth Gospel, in which certain Greeks who have come to Jerusalem to worship at the feast accost Philip and ask to be allowed to see Jesus. Philip relays the request to Andrew, and together they bear the petition to Jesus himself. His immediate reaction is altogether surprising. It is in no way clear whether the Greeks attained their object or not: they are never mentioned again. But it is evident that Jesus regards their coming as deeply significant. It constitutes for him the sign that his hour of destiny has come. The earthly task that the Father assigned to him is almost complete. The Son of Man is about to be "glorified," that is, he is about to be made the instrument of the final revelation of the glory of God. Through him the glory of God will be manifested to the Gentiles and all the ends of the earth will receive his salvation.

There is little doubt that in the eyes of the writer of the Gospel "the Greeks" stood for a type very familiar in the world of his day. The Greeks were beyond all else the *humanists* of the ancient world. They were not enamored with material things as such, nor were they deeply concerned about things that were invisible and intangible. The focus of their interest was man in the ordinary course of his life — how he might attain health and happiness and honor and prosperity. They sought to avoid all that was ugly and repellent and to seek the beautiful and the good wherever it might be found. What wonder that men of this kind who had in some way heard of Jesus should have desired to see him with their own eyes! Could he teach them the way of virtuous and gracious living? Could he show them an example of humanity raised to its highest degree of excellence? If so, they would be ready to cast in their lot with him and to accept him as their instructor and guide.

But not thus could the purpose of God be fulfilled. The universal outreach of the Christian mission could not be attained until Jesus had been " glorified." The Greeks, representing those in all places and of all ages who seek light upon the meaning of life, must find it through a symbol within which death and life, humiliation and exaltation, defeat and victory are strangely intermingled. The corn of wheat must fall into the ground and die if it is to bring forth fruit; the man who instinctively hedges his life round and builds up earthly securities must renounce them if he is to find the secret of life eternal; even the Son of Man must be lifted up upon the cross of shame if he is to gain the exaltation of a universal lordship. These processes are never smooth and easy. The corn of wheat is trampled into the earth, is condemned to months of exposure to the forces struggling to release its inner life, is rent asunder while the new shoot presses upward, and is finally compelled to battle with wind and weather in order to produce its proper harvest. The man secure in the amenities and satisfactions of this life must deny himself and take up his cross and taste a bitter cup and be baptized with a strange baptism and follow the Christ if he is to find the life of the world to come. The Son of Man, so the narrative records, himself must be exercised and troubled. His very soul begins to be torn asunder within him. And what can he say? Will he ask to be saved from this hour of crisis? But his whole career has been moving toward this hour. Did not the Servant of the Lord pass through suffering and rejection and torture and death on his way to being exalted and extolled and lifted upon high? Did he not submit to the lowest indignities in order that the glory of the Lord might be revealed through his sacrifice? So out of the travail of his soul Jesus lifts up his eyes to God and accepts his destiny gladly, willingly. "Father, glorify thy name." In that moment the crisis of the ages was reached. The whole world stood under the judgment of the revelation of the glory of God. The prince of this world stood condemned as his false standards of self-assertion and lust for power and craving for material possessions were exposed to the burning light of the self-sacrifice of the vicegerent of God. And the Son of Man himself, lifting up his eyes and seeing the vision of redeemed souls coming from the North and from the South, from the East and from the West, breaks out into a cry of triumph:

"I, if I be lifted up from the earth, will draw all men unto me."

The glory of the Lord is being revealed and all flesh is seeing it together. The Servant is "glorious in the eyes of the Lord" and is giving light to the Gentiles and salvation to the end of the earth.

So the cross was set up. Even while the darkness covered the earth, faint rays of light began to be seen. The thief sees a ray of glory: "Lord, remember me when thou comest into thy kingdom." The centurion likewise: "Truly this man was the Son of God." And before long the glory is breaking forth until a man is found who cries: "God forbid that I should glory, save in the cross of our Lord Jesus Christ." In an altogether strange and paradoxical way the symbol of lowest shame has become the symbol of highest glory. As we bring this book to a close, we shall seek in a final summing up to suggest three ways in which the cross has come to be a place of glory and honor and blessing and has become the instrument for drawing men of every kindred and nation and tribe and tongue to the feet of the living Christ.

The Triumph Over Evil

From the time of the earliest Christian witnesses down to our own day the Church has never lost the conviction that in some way the cross is *the place of the supreme and decisive triumph over all the forces of evil*. One of the most vivid expressions of this conviction is to be found in Col. 2:14, 15. The passage as a whole is not easy to interpret, but its concluding affirmation is entirely specific on one point. It is that God in Christ gained a complete triumph over the "principalities and powers," and that he did so openly and publicly through the cross. Paul may well have conceived of the "principalities and powers" in ways which we should not find it easy to follow but this need not detract from the force of his central conviction. All evil powers have been overcome through the cross and Christ has won a triumph that is decisive for the whole of human existence.

In a valuable essay on "The Triumph of the Cross," J. M. E. Ross has pointed out that the word "triumph" has come to us with little change from the Greek *thriambos* through the Latin *triumphus*. But what different meanings it carries in Greek and Roman and Christian circles! For the Greek, a "triumph" was a hymn of praise to the god who stirs men's imaginations and passions, and inspires them to delight and even ecstasy through the gifts of the natural world. For the Roman, a "triumph" was a celebration in honor of a public hero who had won a notable victory in battle. Streets were decorated, processions were formed, the spoils of victory were displayed, and the hero himself was feted and cheered as he rode in the place of honor at the end. The "triumph" of licentiousness, the "triumph" of arms — and now, in Paul's daring application of the word, the "triumph" of a cross! All the triumphs were open and public, all were the occasions of rejoicing and exultation. But whereas the Greek "triumph" was a thing of the moment, the Roman an occasional event, the Christian "triumph" was the crisis of all time, the decisive intervention of the living God upon the plane of history. And whereas the Greek and Roman "triumphs" were designed to inflame men's lower passions and to give honor to the powers of this world, the Christian "triumph" was the deathblow to the demonic forces operating in human life and the outward sign that the devil no longer holds dominion over the destiny of mankind.

The question of the origin and nature of evil is one which has tormented men through many generations. They incline always to feel that if only they could explain evil they could control it.

But evil in its many forms has proved the most difficult of all known phenomena to trace to its origin or to follow to its end. How could anything evil have entered into a universe created by a good God? How can there be any certainty of final deliverance from evil? Is evil an inevitable concomitant of material existence or does it belong to the realm of spirit? Is pain as such evil? Are the catastrophes of the natural order evil? Is evil relative to historical progress and enlightenment? All these are questions that have teased and haunted men but to which no certain answers can be given.

When we turn to the Bible, we find hints and suggestions, but no clear-cut theory of the origin and propagation of evil. Yet there are certain all-important affirmations that enable us to face evil with confidence and hope.

The first is that the living God holds the final control over all the forces that operate in the universe which he has made.

The second is that he grants a relative independence to everything that contains the principle of *natural life*. It is the essential characteristic of *life* that it should allow a certain freedom of growth and development. Anything that is completely mechanical and predetermined is not living. Thus, in granting the principle of life to his creation, he granted also certain possibilities of free development, and with this the possibility of perversions and distortions not consonant with the harmony of the created whole.

The third is that he grants a particular form of independence to those living creatures who receive the gift of *social life*. It is the essential characteristic of social life that it should allow a certain freedom of development of interrelationships and intercommunications. That which is stereotyped and automatic and predetermined in all its patterns is not a living society. Thus in granting the principle of social life to certain of his creatures, God granted the possibility of creative progress, but with that the possibility also of excesses and extravagances inconsistent with the wholeness of his design.

The fourth is that, notwithstanding the perversions of natural life and the presumptuous distortions of social life, God has never withdrawn himself from the universe which he has created. Natural perversions may flourish for a limited period, but ultimately they are destroyed by the controlling power of God. Social monstrosities may increase in size and influence, but ultimately they also perish when they stretch beyond the limit of the providential ordering of God. All this, however, is no light and easy process. It is by no wave of a magician's wand that the evil either of the natural or of the social order is brought to a head and destroyed. Rather, it is through the constant travail and sacrifice and judgment and resistance unto blood of the living God himself.

The fifth affirmation — and this is nearest to our immediate theme — is that the travail of the ages has come to a single outward expression in the climactic event of Calvary. All perversions of natural life move toward the infliction of death upon other forms of life. Parasites, disease, beasts of prey, freaks of nature, feed themselves upon the death of living things. Death is their life. So at Calvary death advanced upon the Son of God. In one all-inclusive and representative encounter, corruption and parasitism were allowed to do their worst. Death engulfed him. He was crucified, dead, and buried. But across mankind's " foundering deck shone a beacon, an eternal beam." The resurrection is the life of the Son of God triumphing even over natural death. It is the sacrament of God's final triumph over all the forces that at present mar and disrupt his creation. It is the triumph of the Spirit of life in Christ Jesus over the law of sin and death. It is the pledge to the whole creation that it will be finally " delivered from the bondage of corruption into the glorious liberty of the children of God."

Further we may say that all perversions of social life move toward the infliction of cruelty and force and torture and an iron control over all forms of free expression and creative advance. Imperialisms, tyrannies, dictatorships, rigid legal systems, totalitarian organizations — all strengthen their own sinews by imposing restraint, persecution, torture, death, upon nonconforming elements within their orbit. The repression of others is their own exaltation, the strangling of creativity is the expansion of their own social machine. So at Calvary the political power of imperial Rome and the ecclesiastical power of Pharisaic Judaism joined forces to discredit, suppress, torture, and finally destroy, the Son of God. Systems that represented the overweening pride and presumptuous claims of all forms of excess and extravagance in social life descended upon the anointed Servant of God and trampled him underfoot. He was betrayed, spat upon, mocked, derided, tortured; and if only he had been willing to renounce his faith in a God who transcends all human systems, he could have been released at any time. They bound him once and for all in death; they entombed him; they set a seal on the stone. But " I am Alpha and Omega. . . . I am he that liveth, and was dead; and, behold, I am alive for evermore, Amen; and have the keys of hell and of death." So the cry of defiance rings out in face of all imperialisms and cruel tyrannies. The resurrection is the life of divine freedom triumphing even over the worst excesses of social regimentation. It is the sacrament of God's final triumph over all the forces that at present seek to thwart and nullify his purpose for society. It is the triumph of the Spirit of righteousness and peace and joy over the spirit of pride, vainglory, and hypocrisy. It is the pledge to mankind that the kingdoms of this world will finally become the Kingdom of our God and of his Christ; and that he will reign for ever and ever.

THE FORGIVENESS OF SINS

It is significant that one of the earliest, if not the earliest, doctrinal statement incorporated in a creed is the simple confession: " I believe in the forgiveness of sins." From the beginning the Church has held fast to the conviction that in some way the cross is *the place of the full and complete forgiveness of sins*. In the same Epistle in which he celebrates the triumph of the cross, Paul affirms that in Christ " we have redemption through his blood, even the forgiveness of sins," while in a singularly beautiful section of the Epistle to the Ephesians Christian believers are bidden to be kind, tenderhearted, forgiving one another, even as God in Christ has forgiven them. From that early emphasis upon the forgiveness of God, mediated through Christ's cross, the Church as a whole has never seriously deviated. Sometimes the stress has been laid upon the actualization of that forgiveness in human experience by sacramental means, sometimes by the proclamation of the Word of God. But always the original source of that forgiveness has been conceived as the action of God in Christ, consummated at Calvary. "God was in Christ, reconciling the world unto himself, not imputing their trespasses unto them."

From time to time some leader of public thought arises and tells us that modern man is not worrying about his sins any longer. As a rough generalization, that may be true. Whether, if it is true, it is a good thing is another matter. As Canon V. A. Demant has pointed out, the word " sinner " is a label of responsibility. It is a recognition that man is not a weed or a rag but a being who is responsible to his natural environment, to his social environment, to his own being, and to his God. Weaken the sense of sin and inevitably the sense of responsibility is weakened. Once the sense of responsibility is weakened, how is it possible to prevent the gradual decline of moral standards in social relationships and individual conduct? However vehemently a great thinker like Bertrand Russell may castigate Christians for giving currency to the idea of man as a miserable sinner, the fact remains that the sense of sin is the warning of dislocation or disorder in the system of delicate interrelationships which constitute the wholeness of moral life, just as the sense of pain is the warning of disturbance in the proper functioning of all the necessary elements of the physical system. If man is a responsible creature — and if he is not, his own self-deception is the greatest tragedy of the ages — it is inconceivable that the time will ever come when there will cease to arise from the depths of human hearts the cry, " I have sinned! "

In David Swenson's *The Faith of a Scholar* there is a striking passage which is worth quoting in full. Swenson spent his life as a teacher of philosophy but was critical of all finely spun webs of reflection that seemed remote from the essential experiences of human life. " Who could recount," he writes, " all the miserable subterfuges, the cowardly evasions, the vain and paltry excuses, which in modern literature and thought have been manufactured in order to help the individual evade or escape the sense of guilt? By a curious inversion the problem has been put as the problem of reconciling the goodness of God with the evil in the world, pretending to succeed or assuming to fail in justifying ' the ways of God to men.' This is really but a veiled attempt to shift the burden of guilt from man's shoulders to God's, and to make of the individual a fictitious third party, setting himself up to judge in the case between God and other men, a proceeding as morally fatuous as it is dialectically impossible.

" I remember once to have remarked in conversation with a colleague that there were two kinds of religion: one for good men and one for bad ones; and that I needed the latter kind. The reply was somewhat to this effect: ' But, Swenson, you will never bring the American people to a consciousness of sin.' Far be it from me to have the slightest notion, or the faintest intimation of a notion in the farthermost recesses of my most secret mind, that I have any mission or responsibility in this direction. If this is to be done, the ground will first have to be prepared by abandoning completely this abstract and impersonal notion of being a part of the American people, and substituting therefor an individual consciousness. But even if every other American were an angel, and his conscience pure as driven snow, or if not every American, then at least every American professor of philosophy except myself, it would still hold true of me that I stand in need of a religion of pardon and grace, of a religion that offers and effects a relationship to a divine reality that can reconstitute the integrity of the personality. As a child I was told that I needed such a religion, but I did not at first understand this to be so; later I came to understand it. And now at the age of sixty, having spent a lifetime in the use of such powers of reflection as I have, and in the exploration of my self through experience . . . I still know no better than that what my mother told me was and is the simple truth. But one thing is certain: no man who approaches the God-idea from any other standpoint than from the standpoint of his own moral imperfection will ever have occasion to know the height and breadth and depth of the love of God, which passes all human understanding" (pp. 135 ff.).

Such a confession is of special value for its blunt insistence that the matter of first importance is not the examination of the problem of evil in general nor the concern to establish a universal consciousness of sin. That which demands immediate and urgent attention is the existence now and at all times of *individuals* who " stand in need of a religion of pardon and grace," who crave an assurance of the forgiveness of sins, who long to be reconciled to God. This is no mere conjecture or abstract theory. The pastor in his counseling work, or the psychiatrist in his professional labors, has abundant evidence of the fact. And of what use is it to follow Bertrand Russell's prescription and tell the troubled soul to lift up his eyes and say: " No, I am not a miserable sinner; I am a being who, by a long and arduous road, has discovered how to make intelligence master natural obstacles, how to live in freedom and joy, at peace with myself, and, therefore, with all mankind " ? He may utter the words with his lips and still deep down in his heart the cry will continue, " I have sinned against heaven, and before thee, and am no more worthy to be called thy son."

The question still remains, however, Where is forgiveness to be found? Perhaps the most satisfying answer is that given in dramatic form in *The Pilgrim's Progress*. Christian, it will be remembered, leaves the City of Destruction and gains admittance at the Wicket-gate. But still the burden is on his back, pressing him down and making his journey arduous. At length he comes to a place somewhat ascending " and upon that place stood a cross, and a little below, in the bottom, a sepulchre. So I saw in my dream, that just as Christian came up with the cross, his burden loosed from off his shoulders, and fell from off his back, and began to tumble, and so continued to do till it came to the mouth of the sepulchre, where it fell in, and I saw it no more.

" Then was Christian glad and lightsome, and said with a merry heart, He hath given me rest by His sorrow, and life by His death. Then he stood still awhile to look and wonder; for it was very surprising to him that the sight of the cross should thus ease him of his burden. He looked therefore, and looked again, even till the springs that were in his head sent the waters down his cheeks. Now as he stood looking and weeping, behold, three Shining Ones came to him, and saluted him with Peace be to Thee. So the first said to him, Thy sins be forgiven thee; the second stript him of his rags, and clothed him with change of raiment; the third also set a mark in his forehead; and gave him a roll with a seal upon it, which he bid him look on as he ran, and that he should give it in at the celestial gate: so they went their way. Then Christian gave three leaps for joy, and went on singing,

> " Thus far I did come laden with my sin;
> Nor could aught ease the grief that I was in,
> Till I came hither: what a place is this!
> Must here be the beginning of my bliss?
> Must here the burden fall from off my back?
> Must here the strings that bound it to me crack?
> Blessed cross! blessed sepulchre! blessed rather be
> The Man that there was put to shame for me! "

In these immortal words Bunyan has expressed the essential experience of countless souls. The assurance of forgiveness, the sense of inexpressible relief, the overwhelming gratitude to the Crucified — all these surprisingly and unexpectedly given as men come up with the cross. The " how " of the experience is less important than the " when " and the " where." Yet we cannot altogether avoid the question as to *how* the sight of the Crucified can bring the assurance of forgiveness to sin-laden souls. Can any light be thrown upon this the supreme miracle of man's moral life?

Perhaps the first thing that can be said is that as we gaze upon the scene at Calvary we are convinced that our sin is the *kind* of sin that brought Jesus to his death. Our blindness, our meanness, our self-indulgence, our self-seeking, our refusals to accept responsibility, our attempts to dominate others, our cowardice, our indolence — all these were operating in the hearts of those who brought about the arrest and trial and condemnation of Jesus. If there is such a thing as the shared guilt of mankind, then I had a share in the sin that crucified the Lord of glory. The second thing to be said as we gaze upon the scene is that Jesus' forgiveness is the *kind* of forgiveness that I need. His cry rings out from the cross: " Father, forgive them; for they know not what they do." In that cry Jesus reveals himself as standing by me in my sin and as pleading for my forgiveness in spite of all that it means to him. At the same time it is impossible to think that he was in any way condoning sin or making light of it. Here was no cheap forgiveness, no inexpensive grace. The cross itself is the symbol of what it costs God to forgive the sin of mankind. The third thing to be said is that Jesus' forgiveness precedes any movement on my part to ask for forgiveness; it reveals the great outgoing love of God which suffers through all the ages because of man's ingratitude and folly yet comes forth to meet him and to tell him that all is forgiven. Here is no condescending forgiveness, no forgiveness that has to be "implored." " While we were yet sinners, Christ died for us." " We pray you in Christ's stead, be ye reconciled to God."

Many attempts have been made to penetrate to the heart of the mystery of the divine forgiveness. I do not know of any short treatment that is more suggestive and more enlightening than that of Bishop Angus Dun in his book of meditations on the Seven Last Words, published under the title *The King's Cross.*

"In Christ upon the cross," he says, " we see love of God and love for sinners dwelling in one heart. His love of God does not hold him back from loving sinners. His love of sinners does not stand in the way of his love of God. God and sinners can meet in his heart. They are not, then, hopelessly separated. The life that can take two alienated lives within itself is a reconciling life. Christ's is a reconciling life.

" The forgiveness of Christ came to men with such authority as being the forgiveness of God, because men recognized that he who loved them was the same One who judged them with the stern judgment of God. He did not depart from God in drawing near to them. Therefore they could come near to God in drawing near to him.

" The deepest agony in Christ's passion was the pain of giving such forgiveness. To love purity and love adulterers, to love kindness and love the unkind, to love generosity and love the covetous, to love God and love sinners, that is the inmost secret of Calvary."

Yes, it is because we see a perfect love for God and a perfect love for sinners dwelling in one heart that we draw near to the cross. The Word of the cross says, " Son, . . . thy sins be forgiven thee." The sacrament of the cross proclaims: " This is my blood of the new testament, which is shed for many for the remission of sins." So we believe the Word and receive the pledge and taste afresh the calm of sins forgiven.

> " Blessed cross! blessed sepulchre! blessed rather be
> The Man who there was put to shame for me! "

The Living Sacrifice

The place of forgiveness is also the place of offering. From the beginning the redeemed have made the cross *the place of con-stant renewal of the sacrifice of themselves, their souls and their bodies, unto God*. Because of the unlimited mercy of God through Christ, they are constrained to present their bodies a living sacrifice: because of the love of Christ which passes knowledge they are bound henceforth to live, not unto themselves, but unto Him who died for them and rose again. So the place of Christ's willing self-sacrifice becomes the place of the disciple's oblation. This is doubly appropriate, for it is only in response to the gracious outpouring of the Son of God that a man will offer his life to God; at the same time it is only possible for him to make this sacrifice in so far as he identifies himself with the perfect self-offering of the Son to the Father. We shall glance in turn at each of these two aspects of sacrifice.

1. Catholic devotion has always had two main focuses: the crucifix, and the Eucharistic sacrifice. Protestant devotion has always had two main channels: the hymn and the Lord's Supper. It is easy to point the finger at abuses and excesses in either of these traditions. Many crucifixes are crude and repellent; the sacrifice can easily become almost mechanical in its conception. Hymns have often been mawkish and sentimental; the Lord's Supper can lose all depth of religious meaning. But even when all this is allowed, it is still true that the sacrifice of the Son of God, represented in symbolic form and through ritual drama, has proved able to draw out a response of sacrificial devotion such as no other known action in history has ever succeeded in doing. There are many examples of sacrifice on behalf of a cause; in our own day the lengths to which men will go in costly self-renunciation in the service of such a movement as Communism is often amazing. Men will dedicate themselves to their country, their class, their community, devoting their time and their talents to secure the advancement of the particular cause that has captured their interest. But human leaders come and go, circumstances change, groups disintegrate, and the object of devotion of one age is either forgotten or repudiated in another. This is not the case, however, with devotion to the crucified Son of God. The hymns of the first century still arouse feelings of eager response in the hearts of the twentieth century; the central act of worship of the early Christians is still the central act of worship of Christians today; art forms may change from period to period, but the theme remains the same: He " loved me, and gave himself for me."

Time would fail to recount the long story of those who have found in the cross the motivating power of all their labor of love and patience of hope. Some, as we have suggested, have felt the need of a more concrete, external representation of the Saviour's sacrifice; others have pictured the scene in their imagination and have poured out their hearts in songs of adoration and consecration. Of the latter none perhaps have written more movingly, more authentically, more representatively, at least in the English language, than Isaac Watts and Charles Wesley. It is the great achievement of Watts that in his noble hymn he makes us actually *see* the wondrous cross where the young Prince of glory died. We see the crown of thorns and the mutilated hands and feet, and we know that Watts's response must also be ours:

> " All the vain things that charm me most,
>   I sacrifice them to His blood.
>
> " Were the whole realm of nature mine,
>   That were an offering far too small;
> Love so amazing, so divine,
>   Demands my soul, my life, my all."

Similarly Wesley had the extraordinary power of making us *see* the extent of the Saviour's sacrifice. The blood, the pain, the self-emptying, the death — he touches each in turn with realism yet with great restraint:

> " And can it be, that I should gain
>   An interest in the Saviour's blood?
> Died He for me, who caused His pain —
>   For me, who Him to death pursued?
> Amazing love! how can it be
> That Thou, my God, shouldst die for me?
>
>   .   .   .   .
>
> " He left His Father's throne above, —
>   So free, so infinite His grace —
> Emptied Himself of all but love,
>   And bled for Adam's helpless race:
> 'Tis mercy all, immense and free;
> For, O my God, it found out me! "

In the light of God's mercy and Christ's sacrifice what response can Wesley make save that of glad consecration?

> " Long my imprisoned spirit lay
>   Fast bound in sin and nature's night;
> Thine eye diffused a quickening ray, —

I woke, the dungeon flamed with light;
My chains fell off, my heart was free,
I rose, went forth, and followed Thee."

It would be hard to find anywhere a more adequate one-line portrayal of the Saviour's sacrifice than

" Emptied Himself of all but love."

It would be hard to find anywhere a more simple yet more comprehensive portrayal of the response of the redeemed than

" I rose, went forth, and followed Thee."

So throughout Christian history the picture of the Son of God, suffering, dying, rising, has filled the vision and the imagination of countless souls in every realm of life. Telling how he had placed a crucifix on the central strut of his bookcase as a symbol of the standard by which all works of art and scholarship are to be judged, the late Bishop Hensley Henson, a man who had played no mean part in the world of letters and of public affairs, makes this final confession: " At the end of a long life, when I think over my personal religion, it is still the crucifixion which fills my vision. I see it with the threefold commentary of Scripture, Creed, and History to help my understanding and I add to that commentary the witness of pastoral and personal experience; and still I can discover no more satisfying summary of my personal religion than ' Jesus Christ and him crucified.' " In whatever other respects men may differ, here is common standing ground: He died for me; I must live for Him.

2. Though ready and willing to yield his best to God, man has constantly been haunted by the realization that even his most resolute attempts to make a worthy offering fall far short of a perfect consecration. So easily some motive of self-interest enters in. So often the sacrifice is blemished by an ever so faint desire to win the applause of others. So frequently, as in the case of Ananias and Sapphira, some part of the price is held back. In all too many cases the offering itself is mean and shabby, but at best it is never what it might be. " We make sacrifices," says Forsyth, " and

costly ones, which yet do not draw blood for us. They do not go to the very center of our life. They do not touch the nerve or strain the heart. A man may devote the toil of a self-denying life to a book of stupendous research on the gravest subjects, which yet makes no call on his inmost self and is not written with his blood but only with a sweating brow." How true this is! If all depended on the depth and inwardness of our own self-dedication, our lot would be a sorry one indeed!

But here again it is the sacrifice of Christ himself that gathers up our poor unworthy offerings and sanctifies them by its own excellence. Here is the full perfect and sufficient sacrifice. " What he did," says Forsyth, " drew upon the very citadel of his personality and involved his total self. The foundations of his great deep were broken up. His whole personality was put into his work and identified with it. The saving work of God drew blood from Christ as it drew Christ from God — and not from God's side only but from his heart. Christ's work touched the quick of God; as it touched the quick also of his own divinest life, and stirred up all that was within him to bless and magnify God's holy name." In his case nothing was held back, nothing was spoiled by selfish motives, nothing was remotely related to self-display. " For their sakes," he cries, " I offer myself in sacrifice that they may be consecrated through the truth." May we not interpret this to mean that we can offer any *real* sacrifice only in so far as we become identified with him in the offering of his perfect sacrifice?

In some respects William Bright's Communion hymn may not be altogether satisfactory but the strength of its appeal surely lies in its profound recognition that no worthy sacrifice is possible except in union with the perfect sacrifice of Christ:

> " And now, O Father, mindful of the love
>   That bought us, once for all, on Calvary's Tree,
> And having with us Him that pleads above,
>   We here present, we here spread forth to Thee
> That only offering perfect in Thine eyes,
> The one true, pure, immortal sacrifice.

"Look, Father, look on His anointed face,
And only look on us as found in Him;
Look not on our misusings of Thy grace,
Our prayer so languid, and our faith so dim:
For lo! between our sins and their reward
We set the passion of Thy Son our Lord."

Only within the all-embracing outreach of that one true Sacrifice can our imperfect sacrifices find acceptance with God. The glory of the cross is that it sanctifies the lowliest and meanest and touches it with the splendor of the perfect Offering.

As I draw these studies to a close, I find myself returning in mind to a passage in a manuscript by Prof. D. R. G. Owen, of Trinity College, Toronto, which I read not long ago. The author was concerned to submit the scientific spirit of our age to a searching critique and at one point of his inquiry this is what he said:

"It may be possible to understand a scientific formula without undertaking the relevant experiments (though even here there is no substitution for work in the laboratory) but it is quite impossible to appreciate the real meaning of any of the articles of the [Christian] faith while remaining without faith. It is for this reason that the cross cannot be explained in a book or taught in a classroom. Even Jesus Christ, that great teacher, could not *teach* the meaning of the cross; he had to take it up. Someone once asked Pavlova what she meant by a certain dance which she had performed and the great dancer replied: 'Do you think I would have *danced* it if I could have *said* it?' Similarly if we were to ask Jesus what was the meaning of his death on the cross he would answer: 'Do you think I would have *died* that death if I could have *said* it?' The cross cannot be explained in so many words: it has to be taken up, lived — and died. 'If any man will come after me, let him deny himself, and take up his cross, and follow me.'"

I recognize the profound truth of these words. The cross is more wonderful than all we can ever say about it. The cross makes greater demands upon us than we can ever fulfill. Our only consolation is that the cross holds out to us a succor wider than we can ever imagine or exhaust. We close our meditations with the beautiful words from the Bach *St. Matthew Passion* that immediately follow Peter's denial. This is the point of deepest tragedy in the whole drama. When man behaves like that, where can he look, what can he do?

> " Lamb of God, I fall before Thee,
>   Humbly trusting in Thy cross;
> That alone be all my glory,
>   All things else I count but loss.
> Jesu, all my hope and joy
>   Flow from Thee, Thou sov'reign good,
> Hope, and love, and faith, and patience,
>   All were purchased by Thy blood."

> O God of peace,
> who didst bring again from the dead
> that great Shepherd of the sheep
> with the blood of the eternal covenant,
>   even our Lord Jesus:
> Make us perfect in every good thing
>   to do thy will,
> working in us that which is well-pleasing
>   in thy sight
>   through Jesus Christ:
> to whom be the glory for ever and ever. Amen.
>   — *Heb. 13:20 (adapted).*

REFERENCES

The following books, listed in the order of their use, are sources for quotations in this book.

CHAPTER I

Langer, Susanne K., *Philosophy in a New Key*. Harvard, 1942; Oxford Press, London, 1942.

Milner-White, E., *A Procession of Passion Prayers*. Society for the Promotion of Christian Knowledge, 1950.

Rosenstock-Huessy, E., *The Christian Future*. Scribner's, 1946; Student Christian Movement Press, London, 1947.

CHAPTER II

Dostoevsky, F., *The Brothers Karamazov*.

Hutton, J. A., *The Dark Mile*. Doran, 1927; Hodder and Stoughton, London, 1927.

Macaulay, A. B., *The Death of Jesus*. Hodder and Stoughton, London, 1938; Musson, Toronto, 1938.

Toynbee, Arnold J., *A Study of History*, 6 vols. Oxford University Press, New York and London, 1940–1945.

Davidson, A. B., *The Epistle to the Hebrews*. T. and T. Clark, Edinburgh, 1901.

Aulén, G., *Christus Victor*. Society for the Promotion of Christian Knowledge, London, 1945: Macmillan.

Chapter III

Buchan, John, *Memory Hold the Door*. Hodder and Stoughton, London, 1940. Published in the U. S. A. under the title *Pilgrim's Way*. Houghton, 1940.

Smith, G. Adam, *The Historical Geography of the Holy Land*. Doran, 1919.

Farmer, Herbert H., *The Healing Cross*. Nisbet, London, 1938; Scribner's, 1939.

Montefiore, C., *The Synoptic Gospels*. Macmillan, 1927.

Orwell, George, *Nineteen Eighty-four*. Secker and Warburg, London, 1949; Harcourt, 1949.

Chapter IV

Westcott, B. F., *The Epistle to the Hebrews*. Macmillan, 1909.

Frost, Bede, *The Christian Mysteries*. Mowbray, 1950; Morehouse, 1951.

Bushnell, Horace, *God in Christ*. Scribner's, 1902.

Campbell, J. McLeod, *The Nature of the Atonement*. Macmillan, New York and London, 1873.

Chapter V

Frazer, James, *The Golden Bough* — Volume 9, *The Scapegoat*. Macmillan, 1907–1915.

Forsyth, P. T., *Religion in Recent Art*. Gorham, 1902.

Stafford, T. A., *Christian Symbolism*. Abingdon-Cokesbury, 1942.

Asch, Sholem, *Mary*. Putnam, 1949.

Chapter VI

Ross, J. M. E., *The Tree of Healing*. Hodder and Stoughton, London, 1926; Doran, 1926.

Chapter VII

Bushnell, Horace, *Life and Letters*. Edited by M. B. Cheney. Scribner's, 1902.

Bevan, Edwyn, *Hellenism and Christianity*. Allen and Unwin, London, 1921.

Bonhoeffer, Dietrich, *The Cost of Discipleship*. S. C. M. Press, London, 1948; Macmillan, 1949.

Paget, Francis, *The Spirit of Discipline*. Longman's, 1891.

CHAPTER VIII

Swenson, David, *The Faith of a Scholar*. Edited by Lillian M. Swenson. The Westminster Press, 1949.

Dun, Angus, *The King's Cross*. Longman's, 1926.

Henson, H. H., *Retrospect of an Unimportant Life*. Oxford University Press, New York, 1949.

Forsyth, P. T., *The Cruciality of the Cross*. Independent Press, London, 1948 (1st edition 1909).